Baseball

A Love Story

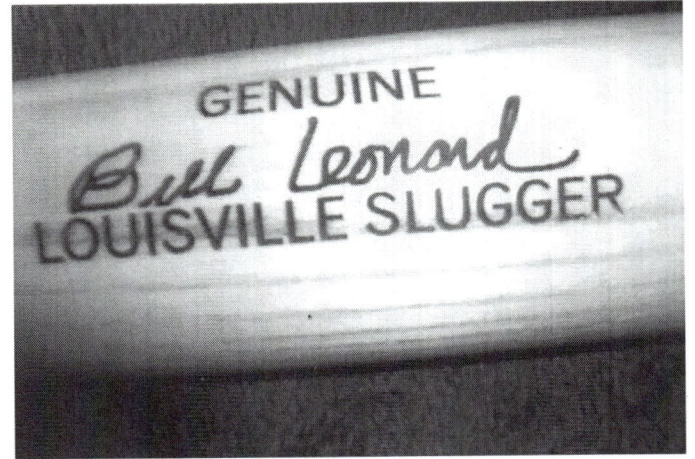

BILL LEONARD

Copyright © 2015 Bill Leonard

All rights reserved.

ISBN: 1508746508
ISBN-13: 9781508746508

PREFACE AND DEDICATION

This is a work of non-fiction with three major sources. One is my memory. Since some of these events could have happened as long ago as seventy years, there is reason to question some details. Others who witnessed the same events might report them in different chronology, have them involve different characters, or even result in different outcomes. I trust that would be rare.

The second source is interviews that I conducted with several local baseball people. Although for the most part they are testifying to more recent events, they too may have forgotten important details, gotten years, or even people, mixed up. I believe their observations are accurate to a high degree. This source is subject to another kind of potential error: deficiencies in my note-taking and reconstruction of the stories they told me. If a factual error is detected in their narratives, I accept responsibility for butchering their stories.

The third source is the archives. Facts and statistics come from recognized print sources. Now and then a sports writer or other contributor makes a factual error. Any retractions or corrections might come days later, if at all, and be missed by anyone relying on archival sources. Those errors can live forever.

This is not a history of local baseball. No attempt

has been made to cover anything before the 1940's, and there was much baseball and many outstanding players long before this account begins. Rather, the stories here begin about the time the position players no longer could throw their gloves on the grass near their stations in the field as they came to bat. Old timers will remember that. Other than the chapter on the Loggers and the stories surrounding the Buckley tours, there is little coverage of the most recent twenty years, a time in which many good local players and teams performed at a high level. This book is just what the title pronounces: A Love Story. If someday a comprehensive history of local baseball is written, I would hope that this book could provide some background and inspiration. A reader who wants to dig into the earliest years could consult George Nelson who has done much work on that time period.

    This book is meant to be part memoir, small part history, and most part recognition and adulation of people who have meant so much to baseball, especially in this area. Not many books list a dedication of nearly 500 people. This one does. It is dedicated to all the people I played for and who played for me, to all my teammates at all levels, to those who umpired, and to those who sponsored and otherwise supported the game, certainly including fans who bought tickets and put change in the cigar boxes that were passed around, to those who wrote about the game, to those who played professionally, and to those who played not very well but who loved the game. This makes any omission of a name in the appendix even more unforgiveable. Not many people have their name in the phone book today. I do. If I missed you let me know.

    I particularly regret that I didn't keep records of the hundreds of boys who played recreational baseball at Memorial Field and at Longfellow. Their joy in the game was as contagious as chicken pox used to be. I hope you enjoy these reflections on the great game of baseball.

Bill Leonard
Onalaska, Wisconsin
Opening Day, 2015

Milwaukee County Stadium, 1956.

BASEBALL, A LOVE STORY

CHAPTER 1

A Love Affair With Baseball

This book is about a deep love for baseball and about some of the characters that touched and were touched by it locally. You will readily recognize some of them; others, like me, were bit players, but we have stories. It's our game. Long may it prosper.

The church of baseball has few converts. It is not a game that can be easily proselytized. Missionaries would have a difficult time selling it, although we had success in Japan. My good priest-uncle's greatest delight was bringing people into the Church. It was good he didn't have to sell baseball. People are inherently attracted to the game. They love it or they hate it.

To many the game is slow and boring. There are no exploding cars or lasers disintegrating the enemy. There is not NFL violence on every play or the end to end fast break action of basketball. Our culture is being immersed in violent and lethal explosions. That doesn't bode well for baseball. It is not healthy for our society either. We have evidence of that.

The unbelievers object to players who scratch themselves and spit. I can explain half of that. The protective cup, worn by all baseball players, can be uncomfortable and is in need of frequent adjusting. That might look like scratching. Understand that, and we have half the problem solved. The chaw is another matter, and one with a long history in the game.

We imitate our heroes. As a boy I would buy a Switzer's licorice bar and spit dark streams between pitches. I couldn't afford many Switzers and I worried about my teeth, so I gave it up. Turk Lown, a Chicago Cub pitcher, used licorice too, but he brushed his teeth between innings, as the television camera poked into the corner of the dugout and documented. A college teammate of mine, Tiny Potts chewed until one day he slid into second base to break up a double play, got tangled up with the shortstop and swallowed everything. He was sick for the rest of the game and chewed no more.

Baseball, in its origins, was a rural game. Its history is populated by farm kids and at a time when a much larger percentage of the population used tobacco in some form. It was easier to chew and chore than it was to smoke and chore. A lot of young players carried that habit over to the baseball field. Organized baseball today knows it has a chewing problem. It is banned in the minor leagues, though not very effectively. There are too many addicted dues-paying members in the union to allow it to be banned in the Majors, but even they were impacted, at least for a while, by the death this summer of Tony Gwynn at age 54.

One of the greatest hitters of all time, Gwynn had a lifetime batting average of .338. He never hit below .309. He was an all-star fifteen times, and, of course, he is in the Hall of Fame. He died of salivary gland cancer. He thought it was from the chewing habit he started at age 18 in his first year of professional baseball. Some doctors thought the type of cancer he had might not have been related to tobacco. Statistically, though, there is an undeniable relationship between chewing and cancers of the mouth. This great game is addicted to numbers, statistics; we base the hit and run, taking pitches, steal attempts, how long a pitcher stays in the game, the use of a pinch hitter, matchups, the lineup, and maybe what is in the postgame buffet on numbers and statistics. It's incredible that we ignore the numbers relating to chewing.

Stephen Strassburg, the modern day pitching phenom with the Washington Nationals, quit chewing the day Gwynn's death was announced. So did Bruce Bochy, the Giant's manager, who used hypnosis in the process. I think a really effective tool would be a tape of Harvey Kuehn chewing. He always looked as though he were in the process of throwing up. My wife, who dislikes baseball, will look up from her knitting long enough to see if Scooter Gennett is chewing or not. It looked as though he quit for a while, but I think he is back at it.

Long ago I was the plate umpire one day for a UWL game. Feisty Mike Dee, a really good local player and now college coach, took exception to a strike I called on him. In addition to the few words he barked at me, he sent a message by spitting toward my shoes. He missed. I should have tossed him anyway, just for coming close.

If you don't like the game, we are not going to win you over, baptize you, and bring you into the fold. On the other hand, the type of love we have for the game means there are relatively few fallen-aways. We baseball fans are steadfast in our loyalty. We have survived the juiced ball, the designated hitter, obscene salaries, inter-league play, and scheduling done by monkeys escaped from random theory labs. Our church has been led by a car salesman Pope who practiced his own brand of nepotism (Selig) and an Ivy League President and poetry scholar (Giamatti). Our greatest threat may have been steroids and we shall overcome them. Of greater concern are the empty sandlots of the young.

Not the least of our challenges among the faithful is the problem of Pete Rose. He is a severely flawed man, the likes of which you would not want your daughter to marry, or even have a first date. But until someone proves that he tried to influence the outcome of a game, in any way except for his team to win, he belongs in the Hall of Fame. If my job were to represent players and their behaviors before St. Peter and the gates he guards, I'd take Rose as a client before I'd take Mantle or Ruth. And they are in the Hall.

Baseball has always been a meritocracy. Cootch Carroll, of blessed memory, who long ago was a bird dog for the Cincinnati Reds organization, tried to get them to sign me to a minor league contract. He told them that the other guys would be out drinking beer and I'd be out running laps. Dale McReynolds, the area scout for the Reds, thought the laps were a good idea but the real question was "Can he hit the 90 mph slider?" Drink some beer if you want to, but hit the breaking pitch. You know how that turned out.

Even the true fan has to choose his spots. You can have my ticket to Opening Day at Miller Park. Yes, it's spring and you know that thing about hope and the human breast. However, too many of those present are drunk before the first pitch. They have paid $35 to turn their backs, literally, to the game and drink $8 beers. They must have failed math somewhere. Daughter Lynn and I waited out a rain delay last September at Target Field, with the home team twenty games out of first place and that hope-promise thing a distant memory. The 25,000 people there watched the game that involved a few September call-ups, some of us keeping score. For us the game satisfies a need for reflection and patience and surprise. Whether in the stands or the dugout or the bullpen, the game is a wonderful venue for storytelling, during batting practice or rain delays or pitching changes. I'd like to take you on a sentimental journey through some musings on this greatest of games.

You will meet some local people you have known, even a few major leaguers. Other characters will run the range from fans to utility infielders to gifted players who climbed a few rungs on the baseball ladder. It will include Dan and Ruth Kapanke and Dallas Ames and Wimpy Miller and Steve Pavela and Sandy Gordon. Rick Boyer and George Horihan will be on the lineup card, as will be Jim Geissner. There will be other names that you would expect, but later. And I am sad to know that I will overlook a number of others, meaningful to me as teammates, coaches, opponents, friends. This won't be an orderly story; it won't be chronological. Baseball is not an orderly game. A 400 foot drive can be an out and a twenty-foot nubber can be a base hit that wins the game. The game might last two hours or it might last five.

Baseball has been a great love of mine. It has also been a distraction. It caused me to cut classes so as not to miss batting practice before home games in college. (I passed the course) I had a college degree before I had a driver's license. There wasn't time to do otherwise. In one college summer, of the roughly 90 days in the thee summer months, I played baseball in two leagues and fast pitch softball in one for 83 of the 90 days and nights. That's how much opportunity there was. It rained the other seven days and nights. I did see seven movies.

Let's begin with a brief local story of a man whose name every baseball fan will recognize.

CHAPTER 2

Elston Gene Howard

Elston Howard played in these environs in 1951. A lot. We know him as a catcher with the Yankees, but he played center field for Bangor in the West Central Wisconsin League. Bill Dickey taught him to catch once he got to the big time. The Yankees signed the 21-year-old Howard in 1950, but he missed the '50 and '51 seasons because he was in the army during the early stages of the Korean War. That's how he got to Camp McCoy and Bangor and that's how a lot of us were able to see this near-legend play.

How good was he? In his 14-year career he was an All Star for nine years. He actually was on 12 All Star teams since there were two All Star games for three years. He played in nine World Series with the Yankees, hitting a home run off Don Newcombe in his first World Series at bat. He was named the

American League Most Valuable Player in 1963. Howard won two Gold Gloves. He had a lifetime batting average of .274. We knew he was good; we just didn't know how good he was going to turn out to be.

As a kid, I saw him play at Copeland Park, not in Bangor where the park, now named Leo Mashak Field, is a notorious band box. One of the difficult things about playing there, and I played there many times, was the thought of how easy it should be to hit one out. I pressed to do that and as a result I never hit a home run there. Batting against Lee Paul and Corky Schilling played into that too.

In the team picture of the 1951 Bangor squad, there he is in the front row. You won't have a difficult time picking him out. Shamefully, the Yankees were the last Major League team to break the color barrier. New York, the epicenter of the financial and cultural worlds of this country, our major city with a diverse population, the home of the Yankees, and the last major league team to employ a Black man. I have always had a distaste for the best team money can buy, and now I have a real reason to dislike them.

The third man from the left in the back row is Casey Davis. The picture was taken at Copeland Park, just beyond first base and before the enclosed and long-gone "Knot Hole Gang" stands. Davis is a very sprightly 84 now, the same age Elston Howard would be if he were alive. He died of a heart condition at age 51. Over a very pleasant lunch at the Village Inn in

Bangor, Casey told me a number of Elston Howard stories. Why did Howard play for Bangor and not the post team? There was a perception that the Post team didn't want to break the color barrier either. However, once they saw how good he was, they changed their mind. Howard continued to play for Bangor, but he would occasionally play for Camp McCoy, for example in the Fifth Army tournament. Add to that the fact that Chapiewski and Mashak and the Bangor "Front Office" were always on the prowl for ringers, who, of course, were paid.

Casey told me a great story about a habitue of the Bangor ball park, one "Clumsy" Schroeder. Schroeder came to the park with money in his pockets and had his own sliding pay scale, so much for a double, so much for a home run and so on. When one of the home town heroes connected, Clumsy would sidle up to the protective wire fence and slip the player a bill. We had a character like that in La Crescent, too, but I never took the money because I thought the donor might be a little too deep into his cups and may not have known what he was doing.

Clumsy knew what he was doing. However, it was late in the game when Howard connected. Who knows, it might even have been the storied at bat when the ball from a Howard drive was found in front of the Catholic church several blocks from the park. I drove there to see if it is possible. The church is slightly downhill from the high ground that surrounds the park. Maybe.

This was late in the game and Clumsy had a $5 and a $20 in his pocket. He made eye contact with Howard, reached into his pocket, and slipped Elston the $5, he thought, a typical payoff for a "big fly". Later at the village Inn, in the ecstasy of yet another win, Clumsy Schroeder set up some beers for a few of his pals. When he reached into his pocket, all he had was a $5 bill. His comment? "I thought Elston was a bit shocked and especially grateful."

Casey, who has an accounting degree from Madison and worked for the IRS must have been a pretty typical resident of Bangor, where he grew up. Elston Howard may have been the first Black person he had come in contact with. He claims that he never heard a racist comment. Before we attribute that to Howard's stardom, remember Elston Howard was a 21 year-old, not yet established as a professional ball player, let alone a star. Often the Bangor team on a Sunday would play an afternoon game and a night game, at least one of them away from the home park. "We had a pretty wild bunch and they would stop at a bar between games and down a few beers" said Casey. "Elston didn't think a player under those conditions should go into a bar, and I was under age so he and I would stay in the car while some of the others downed a few beers."

Both Casey and I, over lunch, wondered if Elston just didn't want to create a problem. Casey said that Howard was always welcome in the watering holes in Bangor. His reputation as a gentleman grew along with his stature as a baseball player. Howard almost never caught in Bangor; Casey remembers Elston behind the plate once. He also can only recall seeing Howard make one error. At Copeland Park, with a runner on third, Howard caught a medium fly ball. The runner broke for the plate. Elston's throw, never seemingly more than head-high, in Casey's words, "just kept rising until it hit halfway up the protective screen behind home plate." If that were so, the paying customers just saw either a miracle or the temporary suspension of the laws of physics. What is sure is that Elston Howard had a major league arm.

The 1951 Bangor team that Howard played on had a 25-year reunion in the summer of 1976. By this time Howard was a coach for the Yankees. Although he was only 46 and fit for his age, he was five years from his death. He graciously accepted the invitation. The Yankees were wrapping up a series in Minneapolis with the Twins and someone, Casey doesn't remember who, picked him up in the Cities and drove him to Bangor. Ryne Duren, the former Yankee terrorist pitcher, terrorist because his eyesight was really bad and his arm was really lively, was the speaker. Duren was available because he was a local lad from Cazenovia, near Reedsburg. He told of a night in Baltimore when he was charged with a half dozen wild pitches and Howard had nearly as many passed balls. Duren really couldn't see those dark fingers when Howard put the signs down. Thus the wild pitches and passed balls. They painted Elston's finger tips and that may have been a first time. Many catchers do that now.

Howard and his wife lived off base in Bangor when he was at Camp McCoy, in a house just up the street from the ballpark. The team invited his landlady, then in her upper 80's, to the evening's affair. Casey told me that Howard spotted her immediately and gave her a big hug. The team and Elston Howard talked long into the night, and the next morning someone drove him to Chicago where the Yankees were starting a series with the White Sox.

Looking again at the picture of the 1951 Bangor team, the player to Elston Howard's left is Dave Hammes, a local legend of a baseball man himself. Dave was a long time game warden and many years later was a neighbor of ours on 19th Street in La Crosse, where we would see Governor Warren Knowles stop by to have Dave take him fishing. Dave and I were both Festmasters and I got to know him well in that role. He was a power hitter and the box score would often show him with a home run.

The man to Howard's right is Earl Ghelf. La Crosse relatives spelled the name "Ghelfi". I am just old enough to have played town team ball against him at the end of his playing days. He was a fiery competitor with a blazing fast ball. These were not politically correct times and bench jockeys could get into Earl's head by calling him " Spaghetti ", an allusion to his Italian ancestry, and an insult. Much of the baseball we played was at night and the lights, particularly at DeSoto, were not good. The dugouts were dim and shadowed. I learned quickly who might shout out the offending word, almost always someone not in the night's lineup. I sat as far away from that person as I could. When Earl glared into our dugout I wanted no chance of mistaken identity. He was not above knocking you down.

When I first started compiling facts about Elston Howard, I wondered if this guy is in the Hall of Fame. He's not. And that is probably a testimony to just how great you have to be to be enshrined. There are only five what I would call modern day catchers in the Hall, names that you and I and fans like us could relate to. They are Bench, Berra, Campanella, Carter, and Fisk. Howard was on the ballot for the allowed 15 years. To make the Hall, a player has to be named on 75% of the ballots the given year. The Baseball Writers of America Association are the voters ,and there are an average of maybe 350 voters in a year. Elston Howard peaked in 1981, the year he died, with 83 votes. He needed 301 that year.

It was a different time, sad in retrospect. While no one could challenge Mickey Mantle's greatness as a player, it just makes one sad to read about him as a person. Jane Leavy's book "The Last Boy, Mickey Mantle" is best left unread. It is dispiriting. But in this book Leavy, who spares nothing in describing Mantle's depravity, says this about his treatment of Elston Howard, the first Black man to play for the

Yankees. " He (Mantle) laid a carpet of white towels at Elston Howard's locker after he hit his first major league home run, easing the path for the Yankee's first African-American player." At another time, Mantle refused to attend a cocktail party hosted by the Cardinals' owner Augie Busch when Howard was excluded.

From Bangor to Manhattan in just a few years. From being Casey Robert Davis' teammate to playing with Berra, Mantle, and Maris. From The Village Inn and $1 fish fries to Toots Shor's, what a ride that must have been for our man Elston Gene Howard.

Seated (left to right): Brady Harding, Jim Warren, Wayne Lottus, Earl Ghelf, Elston Howard, Dave Hammes, Chap Dessner.
Standing (left to right): Bob Spelch, Bunt Blashask, Casey Davis, Bob Arentz, Beaver Mashak, Gene Schroeder, Bob Bjorkman, Bob Steigerwald, Willis Chapiewshy.

Seated Left to Right: Brady Harding, Jim Warren, Wayne Lottes, Earl Ghalf, Elston Howard, Dave Hammes, Chap Dessner

Standing Left to Right: Bob Spelch, Bundt Balshask, Casey Davis, Bob Arentz, Beaver Mashak, Gene Schroeder, Bob Bjorkman, Bob Steigerwald, Willis Chapiewski

Chapter 3

Leagues Everywhere

The heyday of local baseball, the zenith of the game, at least as measured by the number of active teams and players and attendance at the games, was about the turn of the decade, from 1949 to 1953 or so. This book is not a history of the local game, but it will delve into certain periods and this is one of them. Appropriately, a love story doesn't cover everything in a relationship. It does celebrate the highs and regret the lows. This high point of the game was spawned by a perfect storm. People here did not have access to television. The still recovering economy limited peoples' entertainment choices. No other sport had the popularity baseball had. It was American and we were celebrating America, which had recently saved the world.

An objective measurement of that popularity was the number of amateur leagues operating at this time.

If you drove the back roads of Western Wisconsin, and all the roads were back roads, you would see that every town and hamlet had an active baseball field. Dwight Eisenhower had seen the Autobahn in Germany, and the seeds of the interstate highway system, which would eventually be named after him, were planted, but for now, all roads went by a ballpark.

Here are most of the leagues that were in operation. I may have overlooked one or two, and they changed shape and content over these few years. Some teams played in more than one league, and most teams played exhibition games against nines from other circuits. Like shooting stars, these leagues and teams fizzled and died out as the 1950's wore on and society changed. If it were not for Larry Lawrynk and the Mississippi Valley League, amateur baseball might have died out. It might yet, God forbid.

La Crosse City League: American Legion, CIO, AFL, VFW, Onalaska, La Crescent.

This league played most if not all of its games at Copeland Park. Some of the games were broadcast on local radio. Season tickets were sold and there were "Ladies' Nights" from time to time. There is some evidence that an individual ticket cost 50 cents. The plate umpire wore coat and tie and used an outside or "balloon" protector. I came across a sports page picture of an umpire so dressed, officiating at the exchange of lineup cards. I'm sure they also covered the ground rules, including what would happen if a ball rattled off the lumber yard warehouse just off the foul line in the right field corner. There was a lumber yard there! It was 298 at the right field foul pole, 336 in left and 424 to dead center. Those dimensions and my army serial number are taking up valuable space in a data bank that is becoming less and less reliable. I remember a round bell appended to the outside of the elevated press box. It was struck to announce the end of the time allotted to each team for batting practice.

West Central Wisconsin League: La Crosse Mohawks, Bangor, AFL, Holmen, Sparta, Tomah, Black River Falls, Camp McCoy, and Adams Friendship.

The Mohawks featured some interesting roster names. Jim Temp, the Aquinas athlete who played football for the Badgers and had a good career as a defensive end for the Green Bay Packers, was a Mohawk. They imported a double play combination from the Twin Cities, Voss and Clark. Bill Skemp and George Sladky played for them. The Mohawk story could be a book by itself, as could that of the La Crosse Blackhawks, a professional team and part of organized baseball and who played much earlier than this time period. There were interesting stories, I'm sure, about the other teams in the league, but it's the Mohawks I remember. We don't remember, or care to remember, everything about our love stories.

The Little Eight League:
With that moniker, give them credit for modesty. At one point the teams in that league were:
Coon Valley, Cashton, Bangor, Melrose, Onalaska, Holmen, Mindoro, West Salem

It might be a challenge to find the actual sites where Onalaska, Holmen, and Mindoro played their games. The other five fields are still visible and several are still in use. For the size of the communities, Coon Valley, Cashton, and Bangor were all hot beds of baseball. One of them produced a modern day major leaguer, one of several we will meet.

The Monroe County League: Tomah, Cataract, Wilton, Ontario, Sparta, and Melvina.

Tomah and Sparta would seem to be misplaced in this league, being substantially larger communities than the others.

The Wildcat League
I don't know for how long this league existed and there must have been more than the five teams I could find mention of: Hillsboro, Kendall, Clifton, Camp Douglas and Norwalk. I played several games for Camp Douglas; I'm not sure how I got hooked up with them, probably through the friendship of fellow 32nd Division National Guardsmen. I could only play

on Sunday afternoons when La Crescent and West Salem both had night games.

The Norwalk field was "open", that is, it had no fences. That was rare, but there were several parks like that. I was not a power hitter, but, playing for Camp Douglas, I did hit a drive one day that went across the road and into a corn field. I pulled a hamstring at about second base. You might be able to picture Kirk Gibson running on one leg. He didn't have to hurry because he hit it out; my ball was still technically in play. You will also be able to picture a guy who looked like Shoeless Joe Jackson coming out of the cornfield throwing. He hit the relay man perfectly and I was out by ten feet at the plate. Arnie Degenhardt, a catcher of local renown, applied the coup de grace. Whenever I saw Arnie later, he gave me a hard time about hitting one that far and being an easy out.

The Western Wisconsin League: South Ridge, De Soto, Gays Mills, Prairie Du Chien, Stoddard, Viroqua, Soldiers Grove, and Westby.

By the late 50's many of the leagues had collapsed, disappeared, or consolidated with other leagues as town team baseball became less a factor in community life. By the time I played in the league South Ridge, Gays Mills, Prairie Du Chien, and Stoddard were no longer in that loop. Others filled the gaps, West Salem, Westby, Onalaska, and

Melrose. In its consolidated form, the league had good pitching. Lee Paul and Corky Schillings were two of the best. Soldiers Grove threw Eli Crogan and Mark Dilley, who played shortstop for the Badgers in the Big 10 but often pitched for the Iverson boys in Soldiers Grove. This is a painful reminder that the University of Wisconsin dropped baseball. Shame on them. Merlin Nehring, having been released by the Yankee organization, pitched for Onalaska. Everett Johnson had a cup of coffee with Cincinnati Reds and he caught for Onalaska. At West Salem we had several pitchers who make for good stories.

Karl Haverly was our ace and he was a hard throwing right hander who played professionally in the St. Louis Cardinal organization. His catcher in the low minors was Tim McCarver, major league catcher eventually and later a television network baseball announcer of many words. When Karl was through with pro ball he played with us. Charitably, let's just say Karl was not a fitness freak. For at least three innings he would overpower hitters in our league and then he would falter a bit. He would call me to the mound and always say the same thing " Billy, I'm going to load'er up."

Unless you've thrown one, caught one, or tried to hit one, you might not know about a spitball. Here is the simplest way I can describe it. A knuckleball, which is more or less pushed toward the plate from a grip that applies knuckles and fingernails, is an effective pitch because it darts around unpredictably.

It doesn't spin and so even tiny air currents cause it to bob and weave. You have to see it to believe it. It can be very effective, but in a sense it is not as lethal as a spitter because it can't be thrown hard. It is almost pushed toward the plate. There is no spin.

The spitball, on the other hand, can be thrown as hard as the pitcher can throw. When Karl would "load'er up" with the sweat and maybe a little hair oil that were oozing from his head, the ball would usually have that slick spot on it and when it hit an air current it would have a little spasm and move just enough to throw the hitter off. Most hitters didn't even realize it was a spitter. It was just that "Old Karl had good stuff", a lively ball. A spitter does once what a knuckleball does a number of times on the way to the plate and that makes it effective, dangerous, and illegal.

Gene Osgood, a wonderful man who has gone to his reward, pitched for us and almost every pitch was a knuckleball. I'd call for a fastball or a curve now and then, but I'd ask him to throw it for show, out of the strike zone. Gene had a tremendous knuckler and two days later I'd have little bruises all over my lower torso and upper legs. I probably caught him as much with my body as I did with my glove. John Ankney was a hard-throwing lefty for us, and we'll hear about him later.

The Coulee League: Melvina, St. Mary's, Coon Valley, Rockland, Kirby, and at one time, Norwalk

These teams shifted around over a five-year period. I don't know when or how Middle Ridge, for example, fit into the picture. One evening not long ago, going to the church supper at Middle Ridge I noticed the baseball field across the highway from the church. It was a ghost field, overgrown. Like a lot of our memories, it seemed smaller somehow. The plot didn't look big enough for baseball and the field, sitting on the spine of this Highway 33 ridge, had a slant to it. I waited for a while to see if any wool-suited specters, hats at an angle and without sanitary hose, would materialize out of the enveloping darkness. They didn't. But good players played here.

One league I played a lot in was the Houston-Fillmore County League, nee the Root River League. Originally it was La Crescent, Nodine, Black Hammer, Freeburg, Houston, Eitzen, Caledonia and Brownsville. The first town team homerun I ever hit was at Eitzen, over a hedge that served as a fence in a rather short right field. Last summer Kay and I and one daughter were on a country ramble, taking back roads to Horsfalls' variety store in Lansing, maybe the ninth wonder of the world. I sought out the site of the old park to show them this historic, now inactive, field. I was embarrassed to see what a short opposite field shot this was.

Most of those teams were replaced by Mabel, Canton, Rushford, Harmony, Hokah, and Spring Grove. Ron Ekker, who coached the La Crosse Catbirds in the Continental Basketball Association, pitched for either Mabel or Canton. Memory dims. But there was a homerun in this league that I will never forget and it was hit at Rushford by Charley Boma, our first baseman on the La Crescent team. Charley is a big man and he had serious power. Left handed hitters usually like the pitch to be down and in. Charley hit a number of four-baggers for us but this one was a confluence of a perfect swing, contact on the barrel of the bat, sweet physics all around. I've never seen anyone in amateur ball hit one farther. It was probably 315 feet down the right field line, maybe another 20 feet to the adjacent football sideline, then the 150 foot width of the football field, a narrow street and a garden. The ball landed in the garden. Dick Papenfuss will attest to the claim. Charley never again hit one anywhere near that far. Amateur baseball in Southeast Minnesota was well organized. Someone published a multi-page weekly broad sheet at all the parks in the area, covering perhaps a half-dozen leagues. It included the previous week's scores, box scores, individual averages, and some game commentary. We never found out who was behind it, but its editor, under the obvious pen name of "Darby Dicks", predicted the outcomes of each of the games. Even though La Crescent was a perennial league champion, even though we were a consistent winner, Darby Dicks always, always predicted that we would lose. He was very seldom right. We were first miffed and then amused.

    Baseball in all of these leagues went by several

names, for the most part pretty interchangeable: "amateur", "town team", and "semi-pro". These terms were not to be confused with "professional" or "organized" ball which referred strictly to baseball operated by the major league franchises, including their far-flung farm teams and leagues with classifications beginning with "D" and working their way up the alphabet. As time went on the classes "D", "C", and "B" disappeared, replaced gradually below "A" ball by more ambitious college programs and non-professional summer leagues staffed with college players. The Northwoods League which includes the La Crosse Loggers, about whom more later, and the Cape Cod League are the best examples. With one exception, which we will get to shortly, the term "semi pro" was used very loosely. In the very early 50's at the latest, in the leagues around here it was not unusual for a team to "hire" a pitcher, especially for non-league and tournament games. The arrangement might be for $50 to show up and pitch for a team, with a $25 bonus if you were the winning pitcher. Some "semi-pro" games might involve only a pitcher, or maybe both pitchers, being paid. Just before my time, some position players were paid but that practice faded.

    I cannot let modesty get in the way. I have to tell you about the one team that paid me. I don't remember the league and I could only play there when I wasn't playing at night elsewhere. It was the summer after high school graduation and my friend and teammate at Aquinas Bill Schelbe, a left-handed pitcher , and I were paid $5, that's $5 for the two of us, to play for Harpers Ferry, a little river town south of Lansing, Iowa. Bill would borrow his uncle's car and with the $5 we'd replace the gas we'd use on the trip with enough change for several hot dogs and a root beer at some drive-in.

It's important to recall Harpers Ferry because it was there I witnessed the most spectacular thing I've ever seen on a baseball field. It had rained and stormed all night, maybe three or four inches. The morning sun made the humidity almost unbearable, and there were pools of water covering much of the infield. We shoveled water off and shoveled dirt and sawdust in. We put old towels down and wrung them out. We raked the soup. We drove long steel rods into the ground and pulled them out, hoping to drain water. We were soaked with sweat and not making enough progress. In some later day when baseball wasn't as important, someone would have just called the game. It didn't look good for the Mudville nine. One of the team supporters was the local Standard Oil dealer who delivered gasoline to area stations. In a last ditch effort to make the field playable, he opened the spigot on the back of his truck and drove in concentric circles around the infield. He closed the spigot and, realizing the delicacy of the situation, drove the truck out of the infield, across the outfield to the right field corner and a safe distance beyond, coming to rest in a grove of evergreen trees.

Someone pulled the trigger by throwing a lighted cigarette at the infield. WHOOMP! There was what could only be called an explosion. The gasoline fumes had hung in that thick, sultry air. A line of fire the width of the truck zoomed out of the infield (which was a blazing inferno. I think the spigot was more open than the driver thought), roared all the way to the right field fence and stopped. We all thought we were about to see the biggest explosion Harpers Ferry had ever seen. You know how unreliable eye witness accounts can be. It doesn't matter. However close it was, it was too close. We thought the truck was a goner. That would have been 1954.

Just a few years ago Roger Valley, a local baseball nut, talked me into going to Harpers for an old timers game. We had both played there, he long after me. It's against my principles to play those games. I want to remember them and me as we were. As we gathered for batting practice, the stories started. These younger old timers didn't know me, and one of the stories they told was about the gas truck nearly blowing up. As they put it, " the old timers down at the coffee shop still talk about it." I'm not sure they believed me when I told them that I was there.

I promised earlier I'd tell you about a semi pro league that was a little more serious, and that was the fabled Southern Minny. Its high water mark was the late 40's and first few years of the 50's. Teams included the Winona Chiefs, Mankato, Owatonna, Fairibault, and the Austin Packers to name a few. This was not "organized" ball as explained earlier. This was town team ball with paid players. I'll have Ken Blanchard, the Sports Editor of the La Crosse Tribune, explain the problem, which led eventually to the folding of the league.

"The Southern Minnesota league (has) seven of the eight teams operating in the red this season. If the rich Southern Minny teams find it hard to play on a break-even basis, how are the lesser-talented teams around La Crosse making ends meet? Only Austin…is operating on the right side of the ledger. Winona is almost certain to lose money. The Chiefs recently dropped to seventh place, with only a slim chance to get into the league playoffs. Winona club officials were counting on the playoffs to break even this year.. What is the reason for this great expense involved in running a so-called amateur or semi-pro team? Well, besides the usual park, lights, and equipment expenses, the teams have gone into the auction business for players with reputations."

Blanchard and the Winona writer he was quoting go on to float some recommendations: a limit on pay, the pooling of revenue to share with the poorer teams. Sometimes socialism doesn't work; sometimes capitalism doesn't work. In the end, the Southern Minny didn't work.

Before we forget the Southern Minny, we should recount an exhibition game played between the powerful Austin team and La Crescent. I was in grade school and didn't know the game was on in La Crescent or I would have found a way there. It was played right across the street from Dick and Lyle

Papenfuss' house on Elm Street. There have been several baseball fields in La Crescent, the best the present George Horihan Field near the high school. Prior to that, and where I played, was "the pit", now the location of the community swimming pool. The exhibition game was played on what is now the playground of the elementary school. You might not think that possible, but this was before several school and playground additions covered most of right field.

Austin's best player was Bill "Moose" Skowron, yes the Yankee great. In major league baseball he had a .282 lifetime batting average; he hit 211 homeruns and had 888 RBI's. He played in the majors from 1954 to 1967, most notably for the Yankees. He was an All-Star eight times and had five World series rings. In the history of the Majors, he was one of only two players to have hit three game-seven homers, that is, homers in three different game sevens. The other player to do so was Yogi Berra.

He was so outstanding in the Southern Minny that the Yanks signed him. He was from Chicago and went to Purdue on a football scholarship. He played both football and baseball for two years there, and then started his pro career. I tell you this because I want you to visualize a homerun he hit against La Crescent. The field bordered Elm Street, the major north-south thoroughfare. Beyond the left field fence and running east-west is South Fourth Street. The dinger that Skowron hit landed in a tree top across South Fourth Street. The old timers tell me that. They didn't say it went a long way; they were very specific: it landed in a tree top. I did actually play a Junior Legion game on that field the first year I played Legion ball.

In a snowstorm this November, I parked my car on Elm Street and paced the distance from where I thought home plate was in the southwest corner of the lot. I can't be sure where the plate was; all semblance of a baseball field is gone, but I couldn't be far off. At a minimum, it is 450 feet to the street. Then the ball had to fly over the street and into the tree. Is it any wonder that Windy Reider or any of the old boys who saw it, had to enshrine it in legend. This was a strong man with 211 major league homeruns.

For perspective, in 1950 the District 12 Semi Pro Committee – that was our area – sent tournament invitations to 50 baseball teams in La Crosse and the surrounding counties, inviting them to apply for a spot in the tournament. In the paper they said "We know we haven't reached all of you. If you didn't get an invitation, please apply." Their committee was going to have to whittle down the entries to a workable number.

1957 La Crescent State Amateur Tournament Team.

Front: Shorty Olson, Orv Wetzel
Middle: Joe Schubert, Dick Papenfuss, Charlie Boma, Ron Shepardson, Bill Leonard, Lyle Papenfuss
Back: Manager Dallas Ames, Joe Richardson, Joe Gittens, Phil Dahlen, Don Fowler, Darryl Wohlert
Not Pictured: Gordy Bauer

Chapter 4

Twice on Sunday

The two teams I played the most with were La Crescent and West Salem, in the Houston-Fillmore County and Western Wisconsin leagues, and even in their decline, they were the source of many good stories, fuel for the hot stove league. Dallas Ames and Wimpy Miller were the managers, though I played the first year for Al Grob in La Crescent. When the Sunday schedule was serendipitous, it was one league game in the afternoon and the other at night.
Al Grob was a venerable gentleman with a weathered face and a serious mien. He looked like authority. He was the Father of Gary Grob, a teammate, and later the legendary coach who put Winona State on the national baseball map. Al was a traditionalist. In his world pitchers batted in the nine spot and catchers

eighth. Period. It didn't matter what your batting average or your on-base percentage might be, if you were the catcher you batted in the eight hole. In those days I harbored the unrealistic dream of playing professional baseball someday. The guy batting eighth in a summer league doesn't have much chance of being considered a prospect. For that reason, I was glad to see Dallas Ames become the manager the next season.

"Amo" was Mr. Malaprop. He never saw a multi-syllable word he couldn't mangle. He was a scrapper and he expected his players to be the same. If one of our batters had a strike called on a pitch that was borderline low, a call you thought you should get if you were in the field, and didn't think you should suffer if your team were batting, Amo would start the action. He'd bark at the man in blue and then work his way down the dugout, trying to build a coalition. "That was low, didn't you think." There is no question mark there because it wasn't a question. He'd be greatly disappointed if you didn't join him in his umbrage. Dallas would like that word "umbrage"; he'd do wonderful things with it, I know.

Despite his gruff exterior, Dallas was a loveable guy who gave a great deal to baseball, not only to the town team, but also to the high school and American Legion programs. He was past his playing days when I first knew him but I can imagine him in the mold of Don Zimmer or Eddie Stanky or Clint Courtney. For the reader without benefit of baseball history, these were highly competitive players. Nevertheless, Dallas Ames was a caring person.

Early one town team season I played a college game on Friday and then hitchhiked home from Dubuque on Saturday to play a Sunday game with La Crescent, carrying my favorite bat, by the way. Can you imagine getting a ride today, standing by the side of the road with what could be a weapon? If there were rules about playing summer ball before the college season was over, we didn't know about them. This history is so ancient it might pre-date the NCAA or NAIA for all I know. We got rained out on Sunday. Late that afternoon there was a knock on our door. It was Dallas with a $5 bill that he insisted I take to pay for the train ticket for that evening's Zephyr he knew I was taking back to school.

That $5 came either from Amo's pocket or gate receipts that were less each year, while expenses were going up. Let me mention Edward Joseph "Ebba" St. Claire, a backup catcher who spent three years with the Milwaukee Braves around this time and then was traded to the New York Giants in 1954. Ebba was a small part of this trade which brought Bobby Thomson to the Braves. He had a career batting average of .249 and he hit seven home runs in a four year career that ended after the 1954 season.
All baseball bats in all leagues at this time were wood. They broke quite easily, in spite of the constant reminders to "keep the trademark up". They were hard to replace and several times each summer we'd

get to the point where there wasn't much selection to choose from. When things got really tough, a number of us would take the 34-inch Ebba St. Claire to the batter's box. It wasn't a whip-handle bat like a Mantle or Mays, and it wasn't a thick handle like a Nelson Fox or Jackie Robinson. It was just the "Ebba". It looked as though it were made of petrified wood. It didn't have great balance or feel, but it seemed to be indestructible. I don't know what happened to it, but eventually it must have been broken.

Ron Shepardson was our big and profane left fielder, in whose hands any bat looked small. I got to know his son many years later and that's how I came to realize what a kind and family-loving man he turned out to be. He terrified a lot of us then. This large man modified his baseball uniform along the lines of the Cincinnati Reds, sleeveless at the shoulder, only he didn't wear an undershirt. His "guns" were there for all to see. One night Corky Schilling hit the batter before Ron. When Shep came to the plate, he leveled his bat straight out at Corky and said "Governor", that was his favorite epithet and not an honorific. "Governor, you better not hit me." Corky walked him on four pitches, all at least a foot outside. Shep lost his legs and eventually his life to diabetes. Seeing this huge man, at his funeral, reduced to a ceremonial box of ashes, was cause for both prayer and reflection.

Wimpy Miller was the manager at West Salem and the name was not eponymous. He was Mr. Nice

Guy, but there was nothing wimpy about him. I think the name came from a cartoon character at the time, a large man who ate lots of hamburgers and was Popeye's sidekick. Wimpy usually coached first base and Everett Johnson, an opponent from Onalaska, with professional baseball experience and exposure to good bench jockeys, once yelled out to him "Go back to the bench, Wimpy. You are tilting the infield." Wimpy did all the support work. He hired umpires; he dragged the infield; he put the roster together and he arranged the non-league schedule. He sold tickets or passed the cigar box to accept donations. Once in a while he played an inning or two. Long after our baseball days were over we buried this good and kind man.

John Ankney was a left-handed flame thrower who pitched for us. He was wild. One night at Tomah, after I had caught nine innings during the day for La Crescent, John came in in relief. The batter foul-tipped one of his heaters and it went "splat" on my bare hand. It sounded bad but it didn't hurt. The umpire said "Let's see it" and I put my hand back for him. When he said nothing, I turned around and he was backing up looking a little pale. This was not a good sign.

The ball had hit my middle finger on my bare hand and basically tore the finger away at the first joint. The bone came through the tendon; I had a "y" at the end of the digit. It still didn't hurt. They took me to the Tomah hospital where they put a piece of gauze over it and said "Go to La Crosse". My good friend Dick Papenfuss was driving (I still didn't have a license) and he took me to St. Francis where Doctor Paul Phillips was on call. They shot it up and scrubbed 16 innings of batter's bag rosin and dirt off (batters' gloves were not yet in vogue). Dr. Phillips tucked everything back in and sewed it up. When he finished, he gave me several pain pills. " I don't need them, Doc. It doesn't hurt." "Just take them along", he said. An hour or two later the pain was intense and I was glad to have them.

    I was only on the DL about a week and I was playing right field for both teams, praying that no one hit a ball that I would have to turn into a good throw. Batting, it looked as though I was giving someone the bird, with my splinted and healing middle finger straight up off the bat. West Salem was playing in the Wisconsin amateur state tournament and, concurrently, La Crescent, in the Minnesota tournament. It was Saturday in Exeland, or was it Prairie Farm, two baseball hot beds, one of them hosting a playoff game leading to the next round. I was there with West Salem and we got beat.

I had located church and on Sunday morning I went to early Mass and then started hitchhiking to Kellogg, where La Crescent was playing a qualifying Minnesota tournament game. I didn't have a car; I still didn't have a driver's license, in fact. Ad-libbing a route, I crossed over from north-central Wisconsin, through the Twin Cities suburbs and down the river to

Kellogg. I carried a bat on that trip too and it was not an Ebba St. Claire. I got there in the second inning, and got an at- bat right away, sort of a version of the double switch. I felt bad that someone had to come out of the game. This team went all the way to the State Tournament where we lost in the first round 2-1. Gordy Bauer, our legitimate pickup (teams could pick up two players from teams in their region, but they had to be pitchers or catchers) gave up two hits, one a swinging bunt. We had seven hits and lost. But let's talk legitimacy here for a moment.

    The Minnesota and Wisconsin amateur baseball associations had decreed that a player could only play in one state playoff competition. That hit those of us living right on the border rather hard, but that was the rule. There had been rumblings that someone was complaining about someone playing in both tournaments. C'est moi. We had a guy on our roster in West Salem, Curt Cooksey, who didn't play much but was part of the team. The best Curt Cooksey story prior to this tournament year happened in a game he did get to play. He squared to bunt with the bat directly in front of him. He fouled off the pitch which split the visor of his batting helmet, broke his glasses, and felled him like a steer in the slaughter house.

    After we came to his aid, we could see that the cuts were superficial and the batting helmet had cushioned the blow. His glasses were broken and askew, but he had escaped serious injury.. As he was lying at home plate he looked up and in mock seriousness asked "How's the crowd taking it? " But I tell you about Curt Cooksey because once the Wisconsin tournament series started, I played for West Salem under his name. I am not sure who blew the whistle. Probably Bangor. The result was that I received a one-year ban in both states for the tournament series. The pain was mitigated somewhat by the fact that I spent the next summer in the army at Fort Leonard Wood, Mo. Dick Papenfuss might have been caught up in this punishment as well, but if so, I don't think he used a fictitious name. That Curt Cooksey injury reminds me of a John Ankney story that was much more serious, and probably happened a year or two earlier.

It was the big and wild lefty with the strong arm whose pitch rearranged my finger who is central to the story. How wild? In one game that took four hours John struck out 20 batters and walked 12. There were a few hitters who swung just to get out of there. This was a night game at Sparta with a nice crowd in the stands. Dave Benedict or Jim Hilbo may have been pitching for them. That's lost in memory. Cootch Carroll was the plate umpire, and the batter was an infielder named Spink. Cootch saved his life. I know that this game was a year or two earlier than the one the real Curt Cooksey was hurt in, because few if any batters wore batting helmets. There were only a few around and they were not required. The Pittsbugh Pirates were the first major league team to use them. Think of the game pictures you have seen of Williams or Dimaggio batting. They just wore baseball caps. Some players had plastic inserts in their caps, but the coverage and the protection was minimal.

Ankney cut a fast ball loose and it hit young Bobby Spink squarely in the head, making a horrible crack of a sound. I remember clearly saying to Cootch as the two of us bent over the felled player, "Thank God he had an insert". And just as clearly I remember Cootch saying "Bill, he didn't have one." That was baseball on skull.

The ball park went absolutely silent. Spink was down but clear-eyed and in no apparent distress. In fact, he said " I'm fine. Let me up." He said that several times and very calmly. As we documented earlier, these were days when there would be hundreds of fans in the stands. One was a doctor, and seeing the potential seriousness of the situation, he came down to the field. Bobby continued to profess that he was fine. Finally, the doctor said," let him get up and go to the dugout."

A voice of authority in my ear, one I was used to hearing calling strike or ball, fair or foul, said sharply " No! Don't move him." I think the doctor was shocked being countermanded by a mere umpire, though an educated one, an army officer at one time, and a post office manager. Within the next 60 seconds Spink said " I'm really getting sleepy." He was soon unconscious.

He was flown that night, from the Camp McCoy airstrip I was told, to Madison and was operated on in the early morning hours. That summer West Salem played Sparta in a benefit game for him and the Tribune Sports editor, Ken Blanchard, wrote an editorial calling for mandatory batting helmets. Years later I saw him working in the Sparta Post Office. He had a slight speech impediment and a horseshoe scar on the side of his head, but he was alive and well thanks to Cootch Carroll.

For me, broken and jammed fingers, minor spike wounds, and strawberries were constants, to be expected if one played 83 out of 90 days. The strawberries, the abrasions caused by sliding, only healed after the season was over. Not being very fleet of foot, I often slid headfirst, under the mistaken notion that I got to the base a step faster that way. All that really got me was some seeping sores on my lower torso. I only had one serious injury, and that was in fast pitch softball. Most of the local baseball players played in the eight team classic league on Tuesday and Friday nights. Pitching dominated. If you got a man on first with no outs, you bunted. The first and third basemen were close enough to shake your hand. One run decided many contests.

Our Raymond Brothers team was playing our biggest rival, Quality Lumber and Coal in a night game at the West Avenue field. This was going to be one of those great pitching matchups, our Bob Maringer against their ace, Willie Taylor. One run might well decide this contest. How this play got set up escapes my memory but Willie Taylor was on third base with fewer than two outs. The batter lifted a medium fly to right where Danny Beckley was stationed. Taylor tagged and obviously was going to try to score.

Dan's throw was a pretty good one, but it was a little bit up the line toward third. I remember thinking " Hold on to the ball; this is going to be close." The lights went out. Instantly. Maybe there was shock and pain which were erased along with short term memory, but I don't think so. I've many times reflected on what sudden death must be like. One moment you are fully cognizant of things; the next you are in the afterlife.

They had two ammonia capsules in the first aid kit. They broke both of them, one at a time, under my nose and they said I never flinched. You can't completely trust story tellers. I have told people that when they were undressing me in the emergency ward they dropped my metal cup on the floor and that's when I came to. Actually, I remember eventually looking up and seeing the field lights and hearing someone say "He's coming around". I do remember the stretcher being lifted over the snow fence and then being loaded in the ambulance. I lost two front teeth and I had a round bruise in the middle of my forehead. I could not have passed a concussion protocol had one been in existence. Since they didn't find my teeth on the field, I was pretty sure I knew where they were, but I was not going to look for them. I stayed overnight in the hospital and I remember Tommy Larkin the younger, still in uniform, visiting me at the foot of my bed. You want to know. I dropped the ball.

The amazing thing, and I am not at all a tough guy, I had no after affects. No headaches. No Dizziness or nausea. I felt fine and was playing in just a few days. Today it often bothers me when I see young people failing to be grateful, sometimes not even bothering to acknowledge gifts. Raymond Bothers, the housing development firm, paid my dental bills. They didn't have to; I wasn't an employee of theirs. Bob Mehren of First Federal, who was a good player in his day, was sort of our General Manager, I know he had some role in all of this. I'm not sure that I adequately thanked them. I was callow.

Realizing that was more painful than the injury. This is a very superficial look at a wonderful time. I played with Joe Richardson, a thoughtful guy with a lot of baseball talent; I got to play a summer season with George Sladky who had been my high school coach. This summer I had a chance to talk with Bob Maringer whom I hadn't seen in 40 years. I caught his perfect game, the only one I've ever seen or been around. Names flood in, unattached to any particular story, but generating warm feelings, whether they were comrades in arms or opponents: Mike Geary, Bobby Damon, Jack Krull, Billy Richards. It's a bit of a jumble. Maybe that collision at the plate caused more damage than I thought. I'd like to name them all. I'm grateful for their friendship.

Chapter 5

The Mouse Parade

Professional baseball can be a cruel lover. A player's record, even his minor league statistics, are available for all to see. In a romantic relationship one might say " I thought we agreed never to mention that again." It is not so in baseball. Imagine what this would be like in another profession, accounting for example.

Johnny Numbers goes to work at Trane Company, right out of college. He is assigned to gather data for the construction of various department budgets. Through inexperience he misplaces a few items but generally he does decent work and he begins to learn his profession. He gets a "satisfactory' rating on his performance review, earning a promotion the next year to a supervisory position in a small department.

The challenge is greater. Due to errors in some of his work , the company is saddled with several "exceptions" on important audits. Disaffection rumbles down from higher levels. There is expensive rework to be done, and his new manager is not happy. His performance rating becomes " Needs Improvement" . Eventually he is released.
That's the bad news. The good news is that Johnny's evaluations generally don't see the light of day. He moves on, benefits from his mistakes, and does well in another corporate culture. Eventually he becomes a CFO with a corner office and, with close friends, can laugh about his early foibles. In some respects, professional baseball is less forgiving.

The minor league environment of organized ball in the 1950's was harsh. There were at least 35 professional leagues with over 270 teams. The ladder was steep and the rungs slippery. By 2014 the leagues had shrunk to 19 with about half as many teams as in the 50's, yet with a good many more major league franchises. Competition for the public's entertainment dollar was intense. Costs skyrocketed. College baseball became a much bigger factor. Over the four years that I played small college baseball, we averaged fewer than 20 games a season and never got farther south than Missouri. I thought that was just us. Local legend Jim Temp made his mark with the football Badgers and the Packers. Many people forget, or perhaps never knew, that while he lettered three years in football at Madison, he lettered all four years in baseball and was the captain his senior year. Wisconsin had a twenty-something game schedule. College baseball today is a much bigger proposition and has replaced a significant portion of the minor league system. And as long as we are doing a bit of a retrospective here, how quaint is the "letter"? Can you see Melvin Gordon wearing his letter sweater? Nor can I.

The baseball numbers live. Bobby Halaska, an outstanding local athlete, signed with the Cincinnati organization and played in 1958 for the Class D Palatka, Florida, Redlegs in the Florida State League. He hit only .157 as a rookie but showed enough promise to be assigned to Geneva, another Class D team, in the New York-Penn league for the 1959 season. There he hit .270 with eight home runs. We can only imagine the young guns he faced, strapping specimens who threw, in baseball vernacular, aspirins, so-called because that's how big the ball looked coming to the plate. A good percentage of these pitchers had their arms fail. God didn't intend us to throw a baseball hard. It's very tough on the arm, and this was before Tommy John surgery was available. Don't fret for them. In almost all cases their arms work just fine today; they don't use them to go upstairs.

Halaska faced these guys under sub-standard lights. He played with Palatka and Geneva in 1960 and then was out of professional baseball. A failure?

Of course not. He was one of the best young baseball players we've seen around here. His career demonstrates just how difficult it is to make the show, as the big leagues are called. The skill at the top level of baseball is impressive. Even if you are not a fan, you should be able to appreciate a major league shortstop going into the hole, backhanding a rocket, and throwing a bullet to first. There are only a few dozen people in the world who can do this.

An analogy: I once saw Dame Margot Fonteyn, the great ballerina, dance. She was at least 50 years old at the time, hardly in her prime. There were no wires above the stage at the Viterbo Fine Arts Center. She seemed at times to float above the stage. She had unbelievable moves. I had the same feeling I get when I see Andrew McCutcheon play center field for the Pirates. Bravo.

A more down to earth picture might be that of a teammate and sometimes opponent in local ball, Billy Abraham. He signed with the White Sox in 1958 and played with their Class D team at Holdrege, Nebraska. He hit .220, with 11 hits in 50 at bats. He had one double, two triples, and no big flies. That was it. That was his career. In my eyes, it was a great achievement, something I wasn't able to do. Billy was probably representative of thousands of players over the years trying to climb that imposing ladder. In fact, there are well over 200,000 players in the minor league data base. There is an incredible web site that purports to document the records of everyone who ever played minor league baseball. That's the cruelty I alluded to. Our failures documented. From what I can tell, these records are reasonably accurate. Not that there are not errors. In regard to my teammate Art Huinker, and more on him later, he is listed as "throws left, bats left". Art batted right handed, and we always worried just a little bit because when he was at the plate batting right handed, that golden left arm was exposed to an errant pitch.

I might have had a very brief career in Class D, but it would have come at a great price. I graduated from high school in 1954 and there were professional tryout camps all over the landscape. I went to a one-day camp at Mauston, put on by the Baltimore Orioles. I don't remember much at all about the day or how many young players were there or how the drills and game were structured. I think the scout's name was George Hauser, but I'm not sure. After the camp, I was faced with a tough choice.

Still in my possession somewhere is a standard baseball contract from the Baltimore Orioles organization, my ticket to something I had always wanted to do, calling for a salary of $225 month. The problem was I had an athletic scholarship to Loras College. There was no way I could afford college without it. Those fluttering wings, was that the Holy Spirit coming down to tell me what to do? Maybe. I don't remember praying over this. Incredibly, I chose to go to school. I may have reasoned that if I could get a contract now, I ought to be able to get one after playing college ball. There is a startling "rest of the story".

I am going to tell you about Loras baseball and the Mouse Parade, but for now let me just say that I had a rewarding time catching for Loras all four years, after which it became obvious to the scouts and to me that while I was a good baseball player, I wasn't good enough to go very far and so I moved on, playing summer ball and preparing for a teaching and coaching career. Please fast forward to about 1965. I was teaching at Sparta Junior High School and serving as the freshman football coach for the legendary Mike Farley, one of the best coaches in any sport, that I've ever known. Mike's staff was sitting around before or after a meeting, and someone brought up Farley's baseball career, about which I had known nothing. Mike signed with the Baltimore organization in 1954. Start the Twilight Zone theme song.

Hard to believe, I kept my mouth shut. Mike was assigned to Marion in the Class D Tarheel League and had seven wins and four losses. He pitched 93 innings and gave up 98 hits, and he had a respectable ERA of 3.77. That earned him a promotion to Pine Bluff in a Class C league where he went 5-9 with a 5.01 ERA. Even so, in 109 innings he gave up only four home runs. Then, like thousands before him, his arm quit. It almost takes a freakish arm structure to survive snapping off curve balls and throwing fast balls. Mike's baseball career was over. But that's not the big story here. The Twilight Zone music swells.

Farley told a baseball story. I hadn't said anything yet. He told about his minor league camp. " Baltimore was a young franchise and they went around the country signing anyone that might possibly be a prospect. Their strategy was to throw a really wide net and sort out the catch." He went on to say that they were housed in barracks and each morning there were lists of players on the board who were cut, gone after just a few days in camp. Parents and coaches were outraged. Players were stunned. I was stunned hearing this story. I could see my name at the top of one of the first cut lists. The butterfly flaps its wings in South America and impacts me in Mauston, Wisconsin. Eventually I told Mike that we had almost been in the same minor league camp, for a day or two.

    I loved playing baseball at Loras. Art Huinker was one year ahead of me and the team had a record of 47-12 during his four years. He was 19-0. Of course I wasn't there for his freshman year, but I caught all the rest of those games. Art was always in the lineup, playing outfield when he wasn't pitching. Our best year was 1957. The only national tournament for smaller schools was an invitational one in Texas. We were invited. I have never forgiven, nor will I ever, the college President for not allowing us to go.

    Art was a lefty. He had a decent fastball and a decent curve, nothing electric, but he had the best control of any pitcher I ever caught. He'd have me sit with him and watch the other team's batting practice whenever we could. "See how that guy carries his hands? Here's how we will pitch him." And he could put the ball where he wanted to.

He signed with St. Louis after graduation and pitched for Albany in The Georgia-Florida league. He was 6-1 with an ERA of 1.22. He appeared in one game for Columbus in "A" ball, but the data base has no detail. What happened after that is fuzzy. It's been a long time since we've talked. Art was married and had a child. I think he came to the realization that despite those gaudy Class D numbers, it was going to be a long time in the low minors and the baseball paydays were not what they are today. He went on to get a doctorate degree and had a successful and rewarding career as a school administrator.

Shortly after his professional career, we crossed paths a few times in summer ball. He was one of those guys that got fifty dollars to show up and $75 to win.

This was a rich baseball time for Loras. The Loras Athletic Hall of Fame is pretty restrictive and yet I played with six men who are in it for baseball, covering seven years if my math is right. Bill Howie was a senior when I was a freshman. The others, besides Howie and Huinker are Tiny Potts, Dick Breitbach, Dick Wright, and Roman Gales. We had a quality lineup, at times including Potts, Breitbach, Joe Ottavi, and Bob Wolfe. Not one of those guys was much over 5'8", earning them the sobriquet "The Mouse Parade".

We played our home games on the strangest field that any of our opponents had ever seen. Its only positive was that it was in the middle of the campus, easily accessed by students on the dormitory lawn or between classes. There was a huge drainage grate in foul territory not far from third. An asphalt walk crossed the field from the foul line beyond third base all the way across the outfield to the cafeteria. It really spooked the visiting shortstop to go clacking across the walk after a pop up. The left field "fence" was a bank with a sharp drop off. It served the same purpose as a fence. The outfield dimensions were adequate except for right field. It was less than 250' down the line. But we had a ground rule to cover that. The snow fence in right angled sharply away from the foul pole and within 30 or 40 feet became a respectable distance. There was a white flag at that point delineating the difference between a ground rule double and a home run. Hit it out to the right of the flag, two bases; to the left, home run. We were playing UW Platteville one day and they had a left handed hitter named Timmons who had a reputation as a power hitter. We heard he had been offered $30,000 to sign. In today's dollars that would be six figures. I've checked the minor league data base and I can't find a Timmons in this era. Timmons got a pitch in his wheelhouse and hit a monstrous shot, high and towering. It landed on the roof of the cafeteria. Since

I was catching, I had an excellent view, the same as the umpire's. There must have been someone on second, because the call was the plate umpire's. That ball went right over the top of the white flag; not to the right or left, but right over the top.

The umpire ruled it a ground rule double. He had not shown any favoritism prior to this. He had called the game fairly. We were all pretty slack-jawed seeing this gargantuan blow. We won the game. The last out of the game several innings later was a tag play at the plate. I had the ball with the runner still four or five steps away. There was no question about the out call. The Platteville coach was an elderly man who was retiring that spring. At the last out he came from his bench, apparently still steaming about the Timmons call, and just as the umpire removed his mask, he punched him. It was one of the more surreal things I've seen on a baseball field. It was a rather weak blow that didn't seem to do much damage. I never heard what, if anything, came of it.

One of those years our third baseman was Bruno Kowalkowski, a seminarian who lived in the Dominican House on campus. Bruno was a very good natural hitter. He was not a man of the world. One day he hit a foul drive and obviously broke his bat. As he started for the bench to get a replacement, someone said "What are you using, Bruno? " He checked the name on the barrel and said , and I'm giving you this phonetically as he said it, "an Al Kay lean ee". He may not have known Al Kaline, but he could hit.

Don "Red" Jennings, one of our pitchers, told me another Bruno story. We were on the road somewhere. With a twenty-game schedule, we were not on the road often or very far, but we were somewhere in a motel. Don and Bruno shared a room, with two single beds. Bruno knelt by his bed to say his night prayers. Jennings was a spiritual guy and he thought he should kneel down, too, so he did. He stayed on his knees until Bruno finished and then they got in their beds.

Ten minutes later, Bruno jumped out of bed and knelt down again. We have only Red's version of what happened next. He claimed he thought " The hell with it. I prayed once. I'm staying in bed." I was several years ahead of Red and emulating Art Huinker's approach to the game , I was preparing Jennings for his start one day. "Red, I want you to shake me off once in a while. I'll come back with the same sign. It gets in their heads." By the third inning I had to go out and say "Red, I said once in a while, not every third pitch. You are making me look like an idiot."

We were a band of brothers, innocent good guys. I received a solid education at Loras, but the four baseball seasons, fewer than 80 games, remain the most pleasant memories I have. We had several older guys. Bill Hyland had been a Marine in Korea and Romie Gales had been in the service. Dick Wright was our age or close to it, but was a mature leader.

One night, probably my freshman year, we were in a two-story brick hotel in Culver-Stockton, Missouri, with a heavy rope tied to a radiator in each room. That was the fire escape. There was beer on ice in the bath tub and a card game going. No abuse. Just teammates relaxing after a day in the sun.
Suddenly there a loud knock on the door. I, who had never broken training rules including then, must have looked terrified. I'll never forget Dick Wright . He looked right at me and said " Don't worry. I'll take care of it." He did and I don't remember who was at the door, but it wasn't a problem.

One of our trips was to Glenview Naval Air Station just north of Chicago. The day before the game we learned that they were going to pitch Johnny Podres. He had a long and illustrious career with the Dodgers. His major league tenure was from 1953 to 1969, almost all of it with the Dodgers. He missed the 1956 season because he had to be in the service. We were going to get to hit against a pitcher who already had three successful seasons in the bigs.

Even if you recognize the name, you might not realize his numbers. His won-loss record was 148 – 116. He had a career ERA of 3.68. He struck out 1,435 batters and walked 743. His best year was probably 1961 when he was 18-5, but in 1957, his first year back from his military service, he was 12-9, with six shutouts and an ERA of 2.66.

Billy Leonard from La Crosse, catching for the Loras Duhawks, was going to bat, probably only three times, against Johnny Podres. The next day turned out to be one of the saddest days of my life. I was in a bunk at Glenview the night before, not sleeping well in my excitement. I woke to a steady rain, a heavy rain. It rained all day. We had no choice but to pack our equipment and head back to Dubuque. I didn't even get to meet John Joseph Podres. That summer I did get to meet a Giant of baseball, and he had a sharp thing to say to me.

Mention Bobby Thomson, the "Flying Scot", to any elderly baseball fan and he or she will instantly recall the "shot heard round the world", the walk-off home run that Thomson hit at the Polo Grounds against the Dodgers in 1951 to win the National League pennant. It was a most unlikely finish. In mid-August the Giants were 13 games behind the Dodgers, at a time when there were only eight teams in each Major League, and wild cards were only in poker hands.

The Giants won 37 of the next 44 games to tie the Dodgers on the last day of the season. There is some reason to believe that at least the Giants' wins at home were aided by chicanery. Herman Franks, one of their coaches, was in the Giant clubhouse which was situated, oddly, behind the center field fence. Using a telescope, he could easily see the catcher's signals and he used a buzzer to transmit them to the home team dugout. My good friend Terry Collins, local attorney, renaissance man, and baseball aficionado in his role as a volunteer bench coach for

Central High School was employed largely as a sign-stealer. He would have been overjoyed to be able to use a telescope and a buzzer.

    Bobby Thomson denied that he knew that a fast ball had been signaled. Good move on his part. Ralph Branca, off whom Thomson connected, said that he doubted Thomson's claim that he didn't know what pitch was coming, but in a gentlemanly statement added " He still had to hit it". That playoff for the pennant was a three game series. The Giants won the first game and Thomson hit a two-run home run off Branca in that game. The Dodgers won the second game 10-0. Incredibly, the Dodgers led the final game 4-1 in the bottom of the ninth. Here are some grand old baseball names. Alvin Dark and Don Mueller singled. Whitey Lockman doubled making it 4-2 with pinch runner Clint Hartung on third and Lockman on second. Thomson is up and the on deck hitter is a rookie named Willie Mays. You know what happened. The Giants went on to lose the subway series four games to two. So why did Bobby Thomson say a sharp word to me?

    In the summer of 1956 a bird dog from Coon Valley named Olsen conspired with a Braves scout to get a tryout at County Stadium for me and for an outfielder from New Albin named Bruce Ferguson. It would not surprise me if that scout lost his job over this. The two of us were admitted to the Milwaukee club house and outfitted with major league uniforms. Gene Conley, a Braves pitcher and a Boston Celtic, asked each of us what position we played. When he didn't hear "pitcher", he said he was glad to meet us. We took the field hours before game time; the gates were not open and there was no one in the stands. This was such a thrill for me that I was never able to recount what happened and in what order, but I clearly remember each of these several things. In those days batting practice was actually caught by a catcher. Today they just throw to a screen. Del Rice was a backup catcher and he was starting to get the gear on when someone told him " The kid will catch batting practice." He couldn't get his shin guards off fast enough.

One of the pitchers I caught was Bob Buhl, a front line pitcher. He was coming back from an injury and this was the final stage of his rehab. Eddie Matthews was in the batter's box and he said " Give me a deuce, Bobby." At least prior to fork balls and cutters, pitch signals were pretty simple. Although there were more than two pitches, a curve was usually number two, a "deuce". The ball came in straight as a string. Did Buhl not hear Matthews? Then it dropped off the table. I had just seen a major league curve ball. I've forgotten so much about that experience, but I remember being most impressed by Wes Covington. His drives seemed to be jet-assisted.

That day, anyway, I caught while the starting lineup hit, and then the rest of us hit. There was a coach throwing lollipops in there and I sensed that their interest in me waned pretty quickly. We had an order to hit in. Thomson was not in the starting lineup and I happened to be in the order right in front of him. There were a number of rounds. Each hitter got so many swings. In the final round, you got to stay in there if you hit something that would be a base hit. I drove one up the middle and stayed in the box. I drove the next one up the middle, a single in the Houston-Fillmore County League and so I stayed. Thomson said " Get the expletive out of there and let someone who gets paid to do this hit. " It won't take much imagination on your part to know what the expletive was. So I didn't get to meet Johnny Podres, but I had a nice conversation with Bobby Thomson.

Chapter 6

What's In A Name?

Somewhere in San Francisco there is an old car with two bumper stickers, right and left. The one on the left says " Do you know Jesus? " The one on the right says "Yes. He is Felipe and Matty's brother." This is a good indication of the impact that the Alou family has on the baseball world. It may also be a commentary on San Francisco. And, if you are a crossword fan, you have many times encountered the clue for a four-letter word " a baseball family". With one consonant and three vowels, " Alou " is a very versatile word, giving the puzzle-maker flexibility. It's based on an error however.

The family name, the father's name, was Rojas, but the scout who signed Felipe, the oldest and first to sign, didn't understand the Latin culture which included the mother's name in each child's handle. Given her role, that only seems fair. The scout signed him as Felipe Alou. To avoid confusion, when the younger brothers signed, they used Alou.

Felipe played in the majors from 1958 to 1974; Matty, from 1960 to 1974; and Jesus from 1963 to 1979. Felipe's lifetime batting average was .286; Matty's, .307, and Jesus's .280. If you lump the three brothers together they had an astounding 17,473 at bats and they hit .292. In addition, Felipe became an outstanding Big League manager. The three Dimaggio brothers hit an aggregate .298, but that was skewed a bit by Joe's .325. You didn't know there were three Dimaggio brothers in major league baseball? You probably overlooked Vince, the oldest.

    He started the whole thing by running away from home to play baseball rather than do the tough and dangerous work of his commercial-fisherman father. That paved the way for Joe and Dom. Vince played ten years, mostly in the National League, and hit a pedestrian .249. But that's not to be made light of. He was a big-leaguer. Surely you remember Dom? There was one ten-year period where Dom's 1,679 hits were more than any other player's hits in that same period. The next four in order, for that period of time, were Slaughter, Musial, Williams, and Reese, all in the Hall of Fame. There are baseball wonks who think that Dom would be in the Hall but for the fact that he was Joe's brother. They compare him favorably to Richie Ashburn, who is in the Hall. I remember Dom because I became a Red Sox fan listening to the 1946 World Series on the radio. Doerr, Goodman, Junior Stephens, Johnny Pesky, Walt Dropo, Al Zarilla, Dom Dimaggio, Ted Williams, Birdie Tebbets, Mel Parnell, Mickey McDermott, Ellis Kinder, Boo Ferris. You will have to take my word for it that I did that without Googling.

Where I am going with this is the age-old and unsolved question of the relative roles of nature and nurture, and if you are patient, we will apply the calculus to two local families. There are over 300 sets of brothers who have played Major League baseball, and then there are those blood lines that have contributed three sons, the Boones, the Molinas, the Alomars, the Alous and the Dimaggios. Nurture is important and it must play a significant role, but I am going to give an edge to nature: the genes that provide speed, bat speed as well as foot, reaction time, depth perception, hand-eye coordination. The Molinas are of special interest to me because they are all catchers. Mickey Mantle would only confuse the issue of nature vs nurture. His strength and speed are legendary (nature); his father drove him relentlessly, forcing him to bat from both sides (nurture) . I may have omitted a family, but you will remind me. Let's look at one more threesome before we get to the locals.

The Boyers are interesting if only for their

names: Cloyd Victor, Cletis LeRoy, and Kenton Lloyd. Cloyd was a pitcher in the majors from 1949 to 1955. He won 20 and lost 23, a rather nondescript record, including the fact that he walked more batters (218) than he struck out (198). But he was there, and there are a quarter-million plus professional players who never got there. Clete played 16 years for the Yankees, primarily, but also for the Braves and A's. He had 5,780 major league at bats and a lifetime average of .242. That brings us to Kenton Lloyd Boyer.

Ken Boyer was signed to a $6,000 bonus contract as a pitcher by the Cardinals in 1949, in the "bonus baby" era. The signing bonus limit was $7,000, which would require that the player be on the major league roster. In his second year of professional baseball at Hamilton in the Pennsylvania- New York- Ohio (PONY) League his team found itself temporarily without a third baseman and his manager had Ken Boyer fill in until the organization could shuffle the inventory and come up with one. He ended up playing 80 games at third and batting .342. He was promoted to Omaha and officially made a third baseman. It looked as though the Cardinals were a little slow in catching on. He had been 5-1 as a pitcher, but he batted .455.

Courage is another factor in the nature half of the debate. The Cardinals sent him to winter ball in 1954. He was beaned and was unconscious for three days. At that particular time in baseball history he was probably not wearing a batting helmet..

When he was called up he joined, among others, Red Schoendist and Stan Musial and hit .264 in his rookie year. His second year he batted .306. And an amazing statistic, in 1964 he played in all 162 games and was the league MVP. In game four of the World series that year against the Yankees he hit a grand slam, accounting for all of the Cardinals' runs in a 4-3 win. The Cardinals won the series by that same 4-3 margin. In game seven Boyer had three hits, including a double and another home run. Brother Clete played for the Yankees, and also homered in Game 7, the only time in history that brothers homered in the same World Series game. In a rather touching statement, Brother Clete expressed his happiness for his brother's success in the Series. Ken Boyer won five gold gloves playing third. In addition to the three Major League Boyer brothers, four other Boyer brothers played minor league baseball. There are baseball genes. Let's look at two local strains, beginning with the Ghelfi family.

He is not exactly the patriarch, since he is a cousin to the several generations of Ghelfis that grace local baseball history, but we are going to start with him, Earl Ghelf. Earl died in 2008 at the age of 83. As mentioned in an earlier chapter, he was very sensitive about perceived slights to his Italian ancestry. There are those who believe he dropped the "i" from " Ghelfi " to make his name sound less Italian.
Earl played professional baseball for two years, 1946

in the Class C Northern League at Superior and 1947 at Class D Mattoon in the Illinois State League. He did quite a bit of pitching around here later in life, but was obviously a position player in both his professional seasons. At Superior, for example, he played in 29 games and had 95 at bats. That's not a pitcher's line. The records do not show what position he did play.

His two-season minor league lifetime batting average was .195, an "interstate" average in baseball jargon, but before you scoff at that, let me tell you that in local circles he was a man to be reckoned with, just one more example of how good professional baseball players are.

The local Ghelfi patriarch, who certainly inherited some of Earl's genes, and who is more directly responsible for the DNA and RNA of two generations of players after him (so far) is Dick Ghelfi. I caught him for one year in high school a long time ago and he graciously took time to visit with me about baseball. As we sat and talked in his bowling pro shop, I noticed something that never before registered with me. His hands are huge. I'm guessing that the Ghelfis before and after him are physically blessed. Big hands don't guarantee baseball success, but they suggest power, and perhaps other physical advantages as well. This is the " nature " part of the equation.

Dick had a four-season minor league career that spanned classes D,C, and B in the mid 1950's. These were not enlightened times, socially or in the baseball world. Dick Ghelfi was a prospect with an arm that suggested major league potential. I never heard him mention "pitch count" in our chat, nor did his managers concern themselves with that concept. He told of pitching a complete nine inning game on Sunday and then pitching five innings of relief on Tuesday. This is the equivalent of the old time football coach not allowing players to have water during practice. One of his managers in the Cardinal system was Bill Kelley, an old Brooklyn Dodger, who broke cigars apart for chewing tobacco. Another of his managers was Willard Ramsdell, the old knuckle ball pitcher. This was not today's corporate, take-care-of- the- assets approach that carefully monitors pitch count and might require a young pitcher to throw two fast balls and one change up to each batter.

As a nineteen-year old Dick began at Hazelhurst, deep in the extensive Cardinal farm system. He won his first six starts, despite snow squalls the first week and a Neanderthal manager. Somewhere along the line, maybe in spring training, he pitched to Orlando Cepeda and Chris Cannizzero, either very impressive names or meaningless ones, depending on your age or knowledge of baseball history. Near the end, with an arm that suffered much abuse, he pitched for the Class B Beaumont, Texas team that required a bus ride starting right after a night game in Beaumont and ending the next afternoon at 3:30 in Lubbock, Texas, just several hours before the next game time.

Baseball reference sites warn that some aspects of the records of many minor league players are incomplete. Dick Ghelfi seemed to have the record of his career very clear in his mind, and his recollection was very faithful to the archives. He won 33 and lost 29, pitching 447 innings. He pitched in 90 games, 57 of them as a starter. He was nostalgic when he spoke of playing briefly with locals Bill Skemp and Eddie Johnson in the Cardinal organization. With a modern training staff and equipment, and with managers who didn't break apart old cigars, the story might have been different.

Dick Ghelfi was a professional baseball player, a journeyman perhaps, one of only a handful in our area, but a pro. And now nature and nurture come together, first in his son Tony. I never saw Tony play baseball but I saw his athletic ability up close. Darrel Collins, the long- time La Crescent basketball coach, asked me to referee a scrimmage he had arranged with Central High, Tony's school. Dunking was illegal in high school at the time, largely because there were few if any hinged rims. Slamming down on the rim could bend it badly or even tear it down. Very few high school athletes could do it anyway. Tony got a step on his man, slashed to the basket and threw one down from well over the rim. The only damage he did was to the defender's psyche.

Let's dispense with the hard work, the long bus rides, the sore arms all players get. If you want to review his draft details, Tony's minor league career, it's all there with a few clicks of the mouse. Here are the guts of the story, After a steady climb through Helena to Spartanburg to Penninsula to Reading to winter ball, Tony arrives at spring training in the Philadelphia Phillies camp in 1983. His performance is good enough that he has a chance maybe to make the club when they break camp. He pitches five or six innings against the Orioles in the last spring game. In one inning he retired Lowenstein, Cal Ripken, and Eddie Murray 1-2-3, breaking several of Murray's bats in the process. He was assigned to Portland, Triple A. He was a September call up and Mom and Dad got enough notice that they caught a flight to Philadelphia to witness Tony's start against the Giants. He went five innings and got the win 4-2. Spoken like a true Dad, Dick said that the plate umpire, Ed Vargo, was known for two things: a tight strike zone and squeezing the plate on rookies. His next start, four days later, against the Mets, may have been even better, though it was a no decision. The Met's pitcher was also a rookie, Ron Darling, and they got a hit off each other. His third and final start was also against the Mets in the next series, but he was the losing pitcher. He gave up a home run to Darryl Strawberry. But look at this Major League line.

Fourteen strikeouts in fourteen and one-third innings. An ERA of 3.14. A record of 1-1, a hit off a major league pitcher. He never got back to the show. A pitcher's arm and shoulder are vulnerable, and his hurt. Other than that basketball scrimmage and a brief greeting when I saw him with his Dad a few years ago, I don't know Tony. I've worn his shoes though. It must have been painful to contemplate the "what if's". No matter where or when it sometimes ends, a major league career is ephemeral. Stepping on a sprinkler-head hole in the outfield, feeling the arm pop, being hit by a pitch or a line drive, or, like Thurman Munson or Kenny Hubbs, wanting to fly your own plane, those events, and just plain dumb bad luck can end it. It ended for Bo Diaz, Tony's catcher, when he fell off the roof at home installing an antenna. He died. No one, though, can take away from Tony those shining few weeks when his teammates included Pete Rose and Mike Schmidt. Up next is Dick's son, Andy, born two years after Tony. He was drafted out of Indiana State by the Cleveland Indians and played five years of professional baseball. In his first year at Batavia, at Low A ball (D,C,B are gone), he was 2-0 with an ERA of 1.35. He pitched 40 innings, walking nine and striking out 31. It gets tougher as you go up the line. Most of his service was in the Indian organization, but he finished with the Giants. In five seasons he had a won-loss record of 32 and 39, pitching nearly 700 innings. Typical of more modern minor league baseball, and unlike the wringer that his Dad was put through, there were developmental outings that resulted in no decisions. The Ghelfi blood line was there, heart and soul and arm. Brother Nick played baseball and played it well, pitching college baseball at

Stout.

Someday, and it may not be a good thing, geneticists will be able to tinker with the genome system and develop human beings with specific talents and characteristics. That would present great ethical problems. For now, the nature part of the equation seems random, though it is replicated to a degree in several generations. Thus, we have the Alous, and the Boyers, and the Ghelfis. Andy's son Drew was drafted by the Brewers in Round 25 of the 2013 draft and was 2-6 as a pitcher in two Rookie League seasons. Mitch, Andy's next son and a catcher, had the third highest batting average for the pennant-winning Lakeshore Chinooks of the Northwoods League, and plays at UWM. A truism, baseball is in their blood, as it is in the second example of a local baseball dynasty.

Mention the name "Servais" and locals think one of two things, possibly both: a rural neighborhood in these parts known as " The Ridge", or baseball. No doubt there were ancestors playing baseball before him, but let's start with Mark, now 65, though you wouldn't know that by looking at him. He was one of nine children. His brother Dan batted third in that lineup and is the father of Major League catcher Scott Servais, of whom more in a moment.

Mark had an outstanding small college baseball career at St. Mary's of Winona where he played for Max Molock. I didn't call Max a legend because that would be a cliché, and whatever superlative I might use would not be good enough, at least in Mark's eyes. Mark suffered his first shoulder injury playing for St. Mary's and, as he struggled through that disability, a scout came to see him play. Max Molock was a virtuoso with the fungo bat and somehow made sure that Mark didn't have to make any tough throws in an abbreviated infield before the game.

He was drafted in 1971 by the San Francisco Giants, but stayed in school and did not sign. The next year he was drafted, and ultimately signed, by a part time San Diego Padre scout, who, in his entire career only signed two players out of the state of Minnesota, Mark Servais and a guy named Dave Winfield. As Mark said, batting .500 isn't bad. He was assigned to the Tri Cities club in the state of Washington where he batted .326, stole some bases, and broke some hearts, including his own. He had hurt his shoulder a second time and could not throw. His playing career was over. In the past few months, I've looked at hundreds of Class D batting averages. Not many are over .300. I'm guessing, pure speculation now, that in the bowels of professional baseball the neophyte pitchers are young fireballers. It takes a while for the young hitters to develop now that they face strong pitching every at bat. Batting .326 out of the chute suggests potential. We won't know.

Some teaching and coaching, and eventually Mark Servais became a baseball scout, a challenging profession in which he found great success over the last 35 years. The first 20 or more he worked the amateur ranks, high school, college, semi pro. Early on he was asked to go to a big tournament in Michigan. "You better see this young kid, a 6-3 and 185 pound infielder with 'can't miss' written all over him." Those words were from the part time guy who helped Mark, one Hal Newhouser an outstanding pitcher with the Detroit Tigers in his day. In fact, he added for emphasis: " He is going to be in the Hall of Fame someday. Sign him or I quit." The kid's name was Derek Jeter.

His mother was an accountant; she knew numbers and $750k was the number. Mark's organization wouldn't authorize more than $450k. I failed to ask if Newhouser quit. Mark's employer in 1983, I think it was the White Sox, but the stories were coming so fast and I had spilled some of my smoothie on my notes, and I'm not sure. I am sure of this. They were torn between a high school kid and a college kid for the 12th overall pick. Mark said " Take the college kid." They took the high school kid. The college kid was Roger Clemmens. The high school kid has been forgotten. After 20 years of scouting amateur players, Mark's job had a new focus.

The "professional" scout takes responsibility for a number of other franchises and builds dossiers on their inventory for future use. As fans we often read about trades that involve minor league players, for example. It's the professional scout who is called on to know the quality and potential of the players involved: speed to first base, arm strength, hitting capabilities, injury history, pitches mastered, and the very important character quotient, a difficult factor since it can't be measured with a stopwatch. Just as other managers in the business world had to do, Mark had to become proficient with the computer. All of this data is stored for when it is needed.

The scouted subjects include players already playing in the majors, especially the "Rule 5" players. Once a drafted player has been in an organization for four years, he must be put on the major league roster. If not, another organization can claim him for $ 50 k. That is how, for example, the Twins originally got Johann Santana. The rule is meant to prevent the rich teams (read Yankees, among others) from stockpiling young talent and watching it grow old. At a young-looking 65, Mark Servais is dialing back a bit and he now has responsibility for two franchises, nearly twenty teams, and hundreds of players.

Brother Eddie has the baseball genes. He was a three-year All Conference player for UW-L, Co-Captain and MVP his senior year. He taught and coached high school baseball. His resume includes six years as head baseball coach at St. Mary's, and two years as an Assistant Coach at Iowa State. Between and among all that, he started the baseball program at Viterbo. Mark had mentioned that he and Eddie laid the sod on the Viterbo field which in the beginning was across the street from Dairyland Power, out near the seminary. He was umpiring high school summer ball and he noticed this big and "loose" (a positive description of a smooth and athletic ability to move) action on the part of the West Salem catcher. He recruited him for the Viterbo program. That catcher was Damian Miller, who had been thinking of walking on at UWL in football.

Eddie's real claim to fame is the outstanding record he has compiled as the baseball coach at Creighton where his winning percentage settles in at .650. He was the Missouri Valley coach of the year three times and has been equally successful in the Big East Conference, which Creighton joined in 2013. I'm imagining an archaeologist a thousand years from now stumbling onto an artifact identifying Creighton, a school located in Omaha, Nebraska, and a member of the Big East Conference and theorizing that there had been a huge tectonic plate shift. That's enough about Eddie; he is a baseball man through and through.

It's nephew Scott, son of Dan, who made the biggest splash, and is still creating waves as the Assistant General Manager of the Los Angeles Angels. After a solid baseball career at Creighton, Scott was drafted by Houston in the third round, 1988. He made his major league debut on July 12, 1991. In an 11-year career as a solid defensive catcher and handler of pitchers, he hit .245. He parlayed his intelligence and outstanding knowledge of the game into a position as a roving catcher instructor with Colorado, Director of Player Development with the

Texas Rangers, and Assistant General Manager with the Angels.

The baseball DNA in the Servais family doesn't end with Mark and Scott. Mark's son Eric was drafted by the Cubs in the 25th round of the June, 2001 draft. He hit .245 with Boise, in the same league his Dad played, and .299 in the 2002 season, also at Boise. He also played a year of independent ball, high quality professional baseball not affiliated with Major League baseball.

Tyler Servais, a catcher like his Dad, was drafted by the Rockies in 2011 but did not sign. Local fans saw him play for the Loggers and he has also played in a wood bat league similar to the Northwoods League in the mountain area of the West. He caught for Princeton for the last several years and is on course to graduate from that institution with a degree in economics. His baseball dreams aren't over yet, and if he gets his swings into a groove, this switch-hitting catcher could still be seen in the professional ranks. We've covered some exceptional players and families in this chapter, and posited some general theories, at least, about the influence of blood lines, inherited baseball ability. Not all of us inherited ability. Let's look at the larger group of us, garden variety baseball players with a love of the game.

Chapter 7

Gopher Tails and Broken Bats

Parallel to the popularity of town team and semi pro baseball in the 1950's, local youth baseball flourished. It began a downward spiral, I think, when copyrighted Little League came to La Crosse, and elsewhere no doubt, with competitive tryouts, full uniforms, coaching staffs, and night games. It was the beginning of the " let's find the best young players and develop them " mentality. For the rest of you, there is only one right field position. If a team had a grinder, he might be in right field but, more likely, he was on the bench, and soon out of the game.
While I have no data to substantiate it, I think the "open" recreation baseball programs at multiple fields in La Crosse developed a greater number of skilled players, even though that was not the focus of the program. I'm sure it developed kids who were happier

with baseball. There were late bloomers who wouldn't have made the cut in corporate Little League, but who stayed with it and developed. Multiple games during the day gave kids who loved the game the opportunity to fill in when a team came up short of players. There were no league rules against this. There were " field rats " who played several games a day, and, maybe even more important, several positions. For five or six years I worked in these programs, supervising and coaching these young players, but mostly just letting them play. Frequently today I'll encounter a middle-aged, or older, person who wants to reminisce about those days. People who were ten then and are 60 or 65 now are hard to identify, difficult to put a grizzled face and a name together. Grandfathers they are now, who once looked like Charley Brown with a baseball cap with a visor so big that their shoes wouldn't get wet if it rained. You can picture them, I'm sure.

    The field supervisors I worked with were ideal for the job, and not all of them were or had been skilled baseball players. They were educators. Nurturers. Orv Brault and Bob Gowland are names that come to mind, Campus School teachers from the University, then La Crosse State. Bob Schroeder, a junior high science teacher and a very good pitcher in his day, brought a calm and reasoned approach to teaching the game. Terry Witzke and I spent a summer together. He was a teacher and ultimately a highly respected school administrator. He was excellent with kids and he influenced me with his ecological approach. At the end of every day, we watered the grass infield, raked the base paths and tidied up. John Pamperin was with the program for a while. He was a protégé of Orv Brault and he represented all that was good about competition and being a teammate. I will digress to tell you a John Pamperin story.

John was a high jumper and a better than average basketball player at La Crosse Central High School, good enough to play some basketball for the Wisconsin Badgers. Because he participated in track in high school, he only played baseball in the summer, but he was skilled enough to play with our local Legion team made up of athletes from Aquinas, Central, and Logan. I caught, he played first base, and we made it to the State Legion Tournament which that year was played in Hartford, suburban Milwaukee. Baseball is the setting but the point of the story has nothing to do with baseball. It's all about goodness and being a teammate, and the kind of people I would work the playground diamonds with a year or two later.

We were in Hartford for several days. It rained a lot. On Friday the team went to dinner at a decent restaurant, and seven or eight of us, including John and me, sat at the same table. I don't think there were fast food restaurants then. It was a few years later that they began to spring up. Carb loading for energy and how an athlete should eat was a dark science in those days; in fact, it was no science at all. It was primitive. Eat meat. Slay the dragon. I don't think we knew what pasta was. Real men ate steak, and we were told we could order whatever we wanted.

In those days, Catholics didn't eat meat on Fridays. Yes, I know, corporate Catholicism was propping up the fishing industry. I don't buy that, but maybe. Eating less meat wasn't a bad idea though, was it. I was the next to last person to order and the only Catholic at the table. It was steak all around. "I'll have the fish" said I, even though I'm not partial to a lot of fish dishes. It wasn't a particularly uncomfortable moment for me, but John must have thought it was. Ordering next, he asked for fish. There was no doubt in my mind that he was taking one for the team, showing some kind of empathy for the catcher. That's the sensitive soul he was. We, Aquinas, had beaten him, Central, once that season in basketball and I had held him to something below his average scoring. He sought me out after the game with congratulations. I have not seen John Pamperin for nearly 60 years. The last I heard, he was a Lutheran minister in the Seattle area. I'd like to see him again before the last out of the bottom of the ninth.

My partner at the Longfellow site was Don Wolf. I knew what a great guy he was, child-centered, upbeat, imaginative, and an excellent teacher of the game. What I didn't realize is what an accomplished baseball player he was, with the Mohawks and the

Newburg's Men's wear team, among others. He never talked about himself, but fact-checking for this work, I came across sports page stories about his exploits. He was good. He was also a man of integrity so I am confident that the story he told me, the one I am about to tell you, is true.

Don's team, probably Newburgs, found themselves on a Sunday afternoon for a league game with only eight players. These were the days of nice crowds and several hundred people had paid their way into the ballpark. At a time when umpires got no more than $ 10 a game, the receipts were enough to keep the team in baseballs and bats. It was important money. The home team reminded Newburgs of the league rule that a failure to begin the game with nine players resulted in a forfeit. So you lose, Newburgs. However, they were willing to play the game as an exhibition. Two good pitchers were set to pitch, and it would be interesting to see how a two-person outfield, or some other defensive arrangement might work. They could also keep the gate receipts.

Not so fast. Newburgs decided if they had to forfeit, they would pack up and go home. Some panic surfaced on the part of the home team. Hurried negotiation produced the following solution. Newburgs could put the name of one of their absent but rostered players in the ninth spot of the batting order, making this an official game. But that concession came with a price. The ninth player, let's call him Snerdley, would be an automatic out whenever his turn came up. Be as creative as you want with the box score; give him a strikeout, a lineout, a pop up, but Snerdley is going to take the collar today.

The home team may have had the last laugh. Almost 60 years have intervened. I don't know who won the game. Don Wolf swears though that only a few innings into the game, Newburgs had a man on third base with two out and the seventh hitter due up. You can see this coming. They walked the seventh hitter intentionally. Then they walked the eighth hitter intentionally to load the bases and bring the impotent Snerdley to the plate. Threat over. Inning over. This was probably the only time in the history of baseball that back-to-back intentional walks were issued. Don Wolf was a prince of a man. He would not lie.

From memory, and as a guess, I estimated that Don Wolf and I dealt with over 200 players. A story in the Tribune described our program at Longfellow as having 21 teams with 231 players. One of them was Whitey Colburn, one of the fastest running backs that Central High School ever had, and one who would one day be recruited by the University of Minnesota. Whitey was also a good baseball player. He came to the field every day as though his class picture was scheduled. He was immaculate. He looked like a first communion picture. By the end of the day he looked like Pigpen from the Peanuts comic strip. Billy and Bobby Schreiber, on the other hand, more or less started out as Pigpen. They had an active morning before they got to the park.

One day as a game was going on and kids were swarming around, one of the Schreiber boys was sucking on hard candy. Whether he offered me a piece or I asked him for one is academic. He gave me one. It wasn't in my mouth long before I realized there was a hair on it, a substantial hair at that. "Bobby, show me that candy." He pulled several unwrapped pieces from his pocket and they all had multiple hairs on them. The Schreiber neighbors had an infestation of gophers, and they put Billy and Bobby to work reducing the unwanted population. I don't know if they used traps or pellet guns, but the boys were successful. The bounty was a nickel for each gopher tail submitted. The evidence and the candy were in the same pocket.

We had a safety issue emerge and it was Don who had a solution to it. Every time there was a broken bat, and the sound tells you immediately that it is broken, there would be a rush to claim it, often while the ball was still in play. Broken bats were valuable. Add a few wood screws and some electrician's tape and you had a bat for pickup games outside park hours. Don's idea was to save all the broken bats and award them on a special, season-ending day. The idea grew like Topsy. Don and I would autograph them. They would be awarded for special reasons of our own choosing, giving us a chance to recognize some of the boys who, as of yet anyway, hadn't been stars.

One went to the kid with the most freckles; another, to the boy who spent the most days at the park. The kid with the best fish story was awarded a bat. There was an award for issuing the most walks, and one for the biggest smile. Among the contests we had that last day was throwing, both for distance and accuracy, but with the "off" arm, righties throwing lefty. We discovered a few kids who were pretty good both ways. There were actually a few bats given for performance and my old records name Robert Schwertferger, Larry Callaway, Peter Engh, Allan Grinke, Danny Smith, Squeek Clements and Tom Sullivan. All of this must be hard to imagine in an environment where the SUV's roll up and uniformed players roll out. We hit up Coke and Pepsi and Dolly Madison for free pop and ice cream for the advertised big day. And then we made a mistake.

The posters said that there would be a special guest appearance by the King and His Court. If you are old enough, and a ball fan, you know who they were. Eddie Feigner toured the country, the world really, with his fast pitch softball team. He pitched; he had a catcher, a shortstop, and a first baseman. And he took on the best local fast pitch players full teams. This was the Harlem Globetrotters without the Washington Generals, the patsies that toured with them. He kept careful records. The King and his Court won 9,743 and lost 257.

Nonsense, you say. Unless you saw them. They played our big rivals Quality Lumber and Coal , once in La Crosse and once in Arcadia. Feigner pitched to one opponent blindfolded. Struck him out. He pitched to another from second base. Same result. In 1967 in a charity exhibition game at Dodger Stadium Feigner struck out the following in a row: Willie Mays, Willie McCovey, Brooks Robinson, Roberto Clemente, Maury Wills, and Harmon Killibrew. He was for real. His fastball was timed at 104 mph. No baseball pitcher has ever been timed at that speed. And the softball rubber was 40 feet away, not 60. One of Feigner's very rare losses was to Quality in the game played at Arcadia, 1-0.

Local ace Rolf Synoground got that 1-0 win for quality. Rolf had a devastating changeup, so good I'm surprised we couldn't hit it on a second swing. I think most hitters went up there looking for it. I never found it. The game was scoreless in the bottom of the 7th inning with a really good hitter up for Quality, Don Hawkins. Feigner was bearing down and he threw one past Donnie that no one could hit. His catcher couldn't catch it cleanly either. Hawkins struck out; the catcher recovered the ball and threw past the first baseman into right field. Hawkins circled the bases with the winning run.

We must have done a good job marketing our special day at the park. More than a few parents left work to see the King and his Court. An aside, part of the success of the recreation baseball program was that during the day we seldom had parents there. The King and His Court were Wolf and I, each pulling a

wagon with one kid in it. We thought our entrance was dramatic; a few parents thought otherwise.
There was one other local angle. One of the best local fast-pitch hitters I ever saw was Bud Smith, a Northsider who played for Quality. Feigner must have thought so too because the rumor was that after playing here, the King approached Bud about touring with him. Turnover on the Court is pretty easy to understand. You go to work in a different town every day. I have no idea if Bud got a hit off the King or not, but if anyone did, it was likely he. I saw Bud Smith at a fast pitch reunion this year and he confirmed that, indeed, Eddie had inquired.

I will posit a theory: the more young boys that play baseball, the better off are our schools, streets and neighborhoods. And truly sad, how long it took to create those opportunities for girls. It's a double whammy for them, that they entered in Little League mode with softball, rather than the broader recreation model.

Chapter 8

Milwaukee County Stadium

The restful shade of green seats in the massive upper deck, empty of course, should have been an ideal background for the fly ball to center field. I didn't have to move very far to be in position to catch it, and the few running steps I had to make were on the balls of my feet. Long ago a coach told me to run on them or the ball would appear to be jumping and difficult to catch. It was a can of corn, colorful old baseball lingo for an easy fly ball. I dropped it. Butchered it. I might as well have had two boxing gloves on. A base runner, going on contact because there were two outs, scored.

It was August 11, 1957, Milwaukee County Stadium, Cashton against the Milwaukee 901 Club and we got beat 7-4. I was there because Cashton, representing District 12, could pick up players from their region, but they had to be pitchers or catchers, though they could play any position once they were on the roster.

Milwaukee Braves Silver Slugger All-Star game 1956.

I wouldn't want to hurt anyone's feelings about the decision to have me play center field. Surely I wasn't going to supplant Cashton's regular catcher, a wonderful gentleman and excellent, veteran catcher, Bob Wais. Where do catchers play to get their bat in the lineup when they are not catching? First base, maybe, or right field if they are in the outfield. The right fielder needs the strong arm the catcher has, and, in right, he has the foul line to limit the territory he has to cover. On his other flank, the center fielder can cover ground for him. Center field is a key position, captain of the outfield, the fleetest of foot, taking anything he can get to. I had no credentials to play this key position, nor did I have any excuse for dropping the easiest of fly balls. The story line said I had two hits but they didn't make up for giving up a run, nor for the psychological damage of making us look bush.

There is no record of what Dick Ghelfi said when the inning was over. He was pitching, his professional career over, using his damaged arm to keep us in the game against one of the tournament favorites. I don't recall him barking at me; amateur dugouts are usually pretty good that way. He probably never had a professional center fielder drop one this easy on him though. The evening before the game Bob Wais had invited me to dinner, two catchers talking baseball over steaks in a nice setting. It might have been the Hotel Schroeder dining room; it was a white tablecloth restaurant somewhere. He picked up the tab. I hope I thanked him. Other than a few dinners with my uncle, Johnny's on South Avenue had been about the pinnacle of my dining experience. I don't remember much about the game the next day, but I don't remember much about the Eisenhower administration either. It was a long time ago. Playing in a major league park with really good , and forgiving guys who became instant teammates was a thrilling experience.

A year later I got to do it again, this time as a pickup with Sparta, and I remember even less. It's sad that West Salem never won the qualifying tournament. Wimpy Miller deserved to take his team there. We actually won the Western Wisconsin League championship that year, splitting the two halves of the season with Sparta and then winning the playoff game 1-0. Karl Haverly struck out 16 pitching for us and Billy Richards fanned us 13 times. But the District 12 tournament was a separate deal. They made it; we didn't.

Allen Bradley, another Milwaukee semi-pro powerhouse, beat Sparta 6-2. I think I was in the lineup but I can't remember. I was able to find the line score and a paragraph on the game, but not the box score. Virgil Schmitz caught. Connie Gasper gave up a three-run homer in the first inning, but then settled down to pitch well. It's a little alarming that I don't remember much about the game, but how and when I got to Milwaukee for the tournament may have had something to do with it.

I had graduated from college that spring and I still had neither a car nor a driver's license. Somehow a day or two before the tournament in Milwaukee, I got to Dubuque to play in the Dyersville baseball tournament with some college teammates. Dyersville might possibly trigger a memory for you. This small town twenty miles west of Dubuque would one day become the home of the Field of Dreams. That day would be 1988; this was 1958. If you saw the Kevin Costner film, you saw the iconic white farmhouse with the porch swing overlooking the baseball field the farmer had created next to a corn field. Shoeless Joe Jackson and his White Sox teammates would drift out of the corn field and redeem themselves.

One day, still more years later, Kay and I would sit on that porch swing. But this was 1958. The Field of Dreams did not exist. The Dyersville ballpark did, and our team of college teammates got beat in the first round. Art Huinker wasn't there that day. He was pitching in the Georgia-Florida professional league. It was a different age. No cell phones. No credit cards. And personally, without a driver's license, I was still a generation behind even that. My next stop on my peripatetic wandering that weekend was Milwaukee where I was to hook up with the Sparta team. Someone gave me a ride from Dyersville to East Dubuque and the train station. I caught a night train to Chicago, napped a bit in Union Station, and got on an early morning train to Milwaukee. We have never been a nation stitched together by train schedules, but pre-interstate highway days offered some rail options. It's not far from the depot to the downtown hotel where the team was staying. I may have walked. Details of what happened next are wiped out.

I remember pancakes in the dining room of the team's hotel that morning. We didn't dress in the major league clubhouse, rather in some room in the bowels of the stadium. And we lost. My baseball odyssey wasn't over yet, though. I rode back to Sparta with the team, arriving late at night. I'm not sure if someone offered me a ride to La Crosse and I didn't want them to go that far out of their way, or if I just drifted off, but I set out hitchhiking late at night. I accepted a ride to Bangor, which was a big mistake. The intersection of Highways 169 and 16 is in the middle of nowhere, illuminated by a single street light. Very few cars came by in the early hours of the morning. A car stopped. It was Bill Brandt, a fast pitch pitcher and team manager from La Crosse. He took me to my door. It was probably about the time I was standing there alone under the street light that I resolved to move my transportation issues to the top of the to do list.

    I had my first job that fall, teaching and coaching at Mauston Madonna. We had really good kids and good athletes, including Kay's younger brother. That's how she and I got together, a whole other story, and so it was God's blessing. I wouldn't have it any other way. It was, however, a terrible career move. I was the entire coaching staff in this very small school. We were successful, but at that very small school level, with the athletes I had, a trained monkey could have had winning teams. Apprenticeship has its advantages. But the car, and the license.

    The solution was really simple. I went to the local used car lot and walked through the rows of beaters, checking through the windows to see if there was a clutch. Let's keep this simple. The salesman suggested that he and I take the car of my choice, a gray two-door 1949 Oldsmobile with a silver stripe down its sloped back for a test drive, and I drove out into the country a few miles and we turned around. I never did know what triggered this, but suddenly he was a little ashen and he said, very earnestly, " never do that again.". I sensed I had made a big mistake of some kind, but I chose not to bring any more attention to my malfeasance by asking him to explain what he meant. When we got back to town, he asked me to just leave the car at the curb. He said he would put it on the lot later. I bought the car for $ 400 and practiced on the streets of Mauston for a few days. The Driver's License Examiner was the father of one of my athletes and I got my license, even though it would have been difficult for a neutral observer to know if I had parallel parked or just abandoned the car. My hitchhiking days were over.

There is a baseball sub-plot to this segment of the love story. There was no baseball at Madonna, no spring sport of any kind, and so I inaugurated the great game. We had a pitcher by the name of Kaiser who had some previous summer experience and was decent. He was not related to the Kaisers who would play for me at Logan. I rounded up some equipment and some old uniforms and we played. It was easy enough to schedule games with the small public schools in a baseball-rich territory. There was no state association of private schools at the time, but the Catholic schools ran an invitational state tournament. This particular year they had an empty line in their eight-team bracket. We asked and they wrote us in. In one of our final practices before the tournament, disaster struck.

Many of the baseball practices I had been associated with as a kid involved a batting practice pitcher and catcher, a batter, and clusters of guys leaning on each other's shoulders and visiting, all of them hoping that someone else would do the shagging, and so I tried always to have as many people as possible doing skill things concurrently. On this day I would hit a ball to the left fielder and have him throw it to third and turn quickly and hit a fly ball to right and have him throw to the plate. Dave Collins, our second baseman who would go on to have a fine coaching career, wasn't looking as I turned quickly to hit the fly ball to right. I got on top of the ball and hit a line drive that hit him squarely in the jaw and broke it. It scared me to death; I thought I had killed him. Dave's jaw was wired shut and he missed the tournament.

The tournament was somewhere in the Fox Valley, a nice ballpark. We looked pretty shabby, I'm sure. I insisted on sannies and that we wore our hats right and polished our shoes, but we were a sharp contrast to the Milwaukee school, I forget who they were, in the other dugout with their uniforms that were really uniform. Ours sort of got pieced together.

We gained some respect right away though. Their leadoff hitter drove a ball off the center field wall. Our center fielder retrieved it, hit the relay man perfectly, who threw a strike to third and cut down the runner on a bang-bang play. What really made me proud though was that we acted as though we did this sort of thing all the time. It changed the tone of things. You could feel it. Or opponents violated a baseball law, never make the first out at third base. You will hear about another violation of a baseball law later. The third baseman was Wayne Van Ert who would become Kay's brother-in-law eventually. We lost 2-0, or something very close to that.

Our first baseman was John Shelton, who would become the storied Onalaska coach one day. It's almost a fairy tale that a rookie coach in the smallest of schools would be gifted with a competitor of this intensity. Basketball was his best game. I don't think it would tarnish his image as a player to tell you that his vertical leap could be measured with a foot-long ruler and he was not particularly quick. He was, however, the best pure shooter I ever coached, and beyond that, he was the toughest kid I ever coached. I feel safe telling you the following true story because the statute of limitations has surely run out.

There was a time when boxing was an interscholastic sport, both high school and college levels in the state of Wisconsin. Sanity took over and it was eliminated at the high school level. The NCAA dropped it not long after a University of Wisconsin boxer was killed in the ring. Madonna had boxing. It filled the gym and the gate balanced the athletic budget. By the time I arrived, there was no one left to fight, but for one match that had been arranged my first year. That would be the end of it. The Caledonia, Minnesota, Golden Gloves team came to our gym for a match. Some of these kids were out of high school. This was criminal negligence that was never charged. There were several kids in the Vetsch family from Caledonia who were outstanding boxers. At the weigh-in, one of the Vetsch boys registered 180 pounds. We had several football linemen who weighed that much, but they were smart enough not to be boxers. It looked as though this would be a forfeit. John Shelton, a will-o-the-wisp 6'-3", maybe 160 pounds, almost string bean of a fellow, cocked his head in a way that friends many years later would equate to a rooster, and said "I'll take him, Coach." That I let him fight this bout was further evidence of my culpability, and testimony to what happens with beginning coaches who do not have adult supervision. Not many of you are old enough to remember Kid Gavilan and Carmen Basillio, the onion farmer from New Jersey, middleweights, I think. They had several televised fights where they just went toe to toe and hammered each other. That was Shelton-Vetsch. It was like watching a train wreck; you didn't want to see it but you couldn't not watch. John Shelton beat him on all the judges' cards.

My three years at Madonna matched John's last

three years of high school. He played some basketball at UW Platteville. In one of his baseball years at Madonna, we played Aquinas at Copeland Park. Our pitcher had pitched a complete game the day before; I had no one to throw, but before I could ask for a volunteer, the rooster raised his hand. "I'll pitch, Coach." After Aquinas watched him warm up, the first three hitters created a traffic jam at the bat rack. John made Rip Sewell look like a power pitcher, but he was the winning pitcher. All baseball players can recall at least one situation where the opposing pitcher had so little stuff that he couldn't be hit. It was John's day. The down side now was that he thought he was a pitcher.

The problem with celebrating teams, and certainly individuals, is that I will overlook some, fail to mention them, or maybe not even remember some of their exploits. This was brought home to me the other day when I visited with Dick Dahlby at adjoining lockers at the YMCA. Fact checking, I have run into any number of stories about his success on the baseball fields of the area. And then very recently as I waited in line to pay my respects to the family of Doug Martin, baseball memories came charging forward. Doug and I were contemporaries, graduating the same year, he from Logan and I, Aquinas. He was a highly-respected college basketball coach in the state of South Dakota. But it was a picture that got me. It was in one of those displays seen at wakes, and as the line moved slowly, I had time to reflect on it.

It was the picture of the 1945 American Legion baseball Wisconsin state champions, La Crosse. The coach was Rod Martin, Doug's father, and in the front row, there was the batboy, nine-year old Doug Martin. Some of the players were Dick Bradburn, Corky Schilling, Jerry Bendel, Dick and Ralph Twite, and Jimmy Wanner. One name in particular impacted me, Jim Knutson. He must have been a very young player on that team. I officiated for 30 years with Jim and I don't ever recall him telling me that he was a state champion. So many of the outstanding local baseball players of my lifetime were self-effacing standouts. The picture caused me a little angst, allowed a repressed memory to bubble up out of the swamp of things best forgotten. I probably kept Rod Martin from having another chance to coach a state Legion championship team, this one in 1952.

Rod Martin was our coach, the last year he would coach the local Legion team. We were pretty deep into the tournament and we were playing a single elimination game at the old Rock Bowl in Viroqua. They had a banner strung over the main street advertising a coming town team game promising that Pete Gordineer would be pitching for the home team. That storied gentleman died just this past year or so, well into his 90's. But this was the Legion tournament. We were not even playing Viroqua. It might have been Richland Center, but it was the Rock Bowl, with an infield with an unusual dirt surface. It was smooth enough, but it was almost shale.

Bottom of the ninth. High school played seven innings, but Legion tournament games, at least in those days, were nine innings. We were down one run in the bottom of the ninth with one out. Bill Shely was on third and I was on second and we had the middle of the order up. We had lots of ways to tie or win this game: wild pitch, passed ball, flyball to the outfield, something hit to the right side of a half-mast infield, and, of course a base hit, even a seeing-eye single. Rod Martin had been there before. He was taking no chances. He called time out.

He came out to the middle of the infield and called Shely and me together. He reviewed the possibilities and then stressed the one most important to him. He told us that on a ground ball to the left side we were to make it " go through". Good decision. He did not put the contact play on. Rather, if it is a ground ball to the left side of the infield, we were to see it go through the infield before we advanced. He went back to the bench.

It could have been the very next pitch. For sure, it was one of the next several pitches. The batter hit a one-hopper right to the shortstop and Shely, against the direction we had just received, broke for the plate. He was going to be a dead duck. I remember thinking I might as well move up, even though there's not a lot of advantage to being on third with two outs. And now there were two outs because Shely was gunned down at the plate. I also remember thinking that I had better be safe at third. I would have been fine had I just gone straight into the bag. I took a cautious approach and did a little fade away slide to the outfield side of third base, making it impossible for the catcher to throw me out. Remember that shale infield? Tiny smooth pebbles. Ball bearings, really. I might as well have been on rollers. I slid well beyond the bag, my grip on the canvas ripped loose. They had a bang-bang double play and the game and the season were over. Could it have been worse? Yes, I was riding in Coach Martin's car. It was very quiet on the way home, and the 35 miles seemed like 135. Love is great, but it can break hearts.

1957 Cashton State Semi-Pro Team. The author is the man in the back row with teeth missing.

Chapter 9

Two Impossible Games

Some baseball games would make bad movies. They couldn't happen. To succeed as stories, they would have to have some credibility; there would have to be an element of possibility. Let me tell you about two games that could not have happened, but they did.

It is May 26, 1959. The Pittsburg Pirates, winners of five straight games, the first win in that streak a complete game pitched by Harvey Haddix, arrive in Milwaukee to start a series with the Braves. One of their leading players, Dick Groat, is mired in a terrible slump and is benched. The great and future Hall of Famer Roberto Clemente is hurt and not in the lineup.

Harvey Haddix is scheduled to pitch for the Pirates but he is sick, probably the flu. He was tempted to stay in bed in his hotel room, and would have, but for the fact that it was his turn to pitch. He was under the weather, and the weather they would all be under that night was not good: periodic gusting winds, on and off light rain but not enough to interrupt the game, and lightning in the distance throughout the night. It's game on before 19,194 paid fans, including a local Milwaukee car dealer named Bud Selig.

Haddix is an interesting character. Early in his career with the St. Louis Cardinals he was a teammate of Harry "The Cat" Brecheen. They were both pitchers who fielded their positions well, both lefthanders. Brecheen was nicknamed "The Cat" for his quick and graceful moves in the field. Haddix, who joined the Cardinals near the end of Brecheen's career was tagged "The Kitten", for similar skills. They were both relatively small men by today's standards, no more than 5'10" and 165 pounds. Haddix would go on to be a three-time All Star. In 1953 he was a twenty-game winner, and for his career his record was 136-116. He had two wins in the 1960 World Series, including Game Seven, when Bill Mazeroski's walk-off homerun beat the Yankees. His first Major League win came in 1952 against the Boston Braves. The losing pitcher that day was Lew Burdette. File that away for now.

Haddix was a tough out at the plate. His lifetime

batting average was .212, good for a pitcher. He had four career homeruns, and more notably, seven triples in 871 official at-bats. To add a little pathos and bathos to the story, he was a chain smoker. He never stopped. He died of emphysema at age 68 in 1994. It's probably not on his tombstone, but he was quoted shortly before he died as saying " I loved cigarettes, but they finally got me."

This night in Milwaukee Haddix pitched twelve consecutive perfect innings, 36 men up and 36 down. Lew Burdette, the losing pitcher in Haddix' first major league win, battled to keep Milwaukee in the game. He held the Pirates scoreless for thirteen innings. His shutout was starkly different than Haddix'. Burdette gave up twelve hits and two walks, but three double plays and a caught stealing kept him even with Haddix on the scoreboard.

Milwaukee batting now in the bottom of the 13th. Felix Mantilla hits a routine grounder to Don Hoak at third, and Hoak throws into the dirt at first. What should have been an easy out is an error; the perfect game is over, but the no hitter is still in play. To give you an idea of how precious the thought of a run is this night, Eddie Matthews is asked to sacrifice and he bunts Mantilla to second. Henry Aaron is next and he is walked intentionally, the razor-sharp Haddix' only walk of the night, of course. Now Joe Adcock has a shot. Haddix hung a slider, his only mistake in this incredible game, and Joe drove it over the right centerfield wall. That ended the impossible game, and started the confusion.

What was the final score? For a minute or two it was 3-0. But Aaron, after rounding second thought the game was over and he headed to the dugout. Adcock passed him on the base paths and was declared "out" for doing so. He only officially reached second base. In the confusion, a score of 2-0 was posted. The President of the National League ruled the next day that Adcock be credited with a double, and the game was over when Mantilla scored. Braves 1, Pirates 0.

You might think it criminal to let Haddix pitch almost 14 innings, but he only threw 115 pitches. He never threw more than 14 pitches in any one inning. Surely they must have charted pitches in those days, usually the job of the next day's starter, but there wasn't much of an emphasis on pitch count. In today's stadium the pitch count is displayed digitally in plain sight for all to see. In this case, they had to check with Western Union to get the count. Pitch by pitch the games were put on the Western Union wire. I often listened to a play by play announcer broadcast an entire game by reading the teletype. Before the Braves came to Milwaukee, we had only Bert Wilson and the Cubs on the radio. If the Cubs were rained out, a studio announcer did a teletype game. He had a little mallet and he smacked a board so that you could hear the crack of the bat.

It is a rarity for a major league pitcher to throw a complete game today, but if he does, a pitch count of

115 to 120 is not unusual. Elroy Face, the Pirate reliever, was 18-1 in 1959. He was never called on to warm up during this game of games. The Pirate pitching staff threw 48 complete games that year. Vernon Law had 20, Haddix 14, Bob Friend 7 and Ron Kline 7. Compare that to 2014. The World Champion San Francisco Giants had eight complete games, four of them by Madison Bumgarder. The American League champions, the Kansas City Royals, had three! The Twins had two. And one other fact about this impossible encounter: the time of game was 2:54, which is probably about the average for a nine inning game today.

    After the game, Lew Burdette called Haddix, club house to club house, and told him he was sorry that he hadn't won such a magnificent game. Haddix and Don Hoak, the guy whose error cost the game, shared a cab back to the hotel. Ed Sullivan called and offered Haddix $500 and all expenses to appear on the Ed Sullivan show. Haddix turned him down, telling him he didn't want to leave the team. A week later, in his next start, the leadoff hitter hit the third pitch for a single, but The Kitten scattered eight hits and won a complete game shutout. I had a very fragile connection to the thirteen-inning game . I was one of several basic training recruits standing around a bunk at Fort Leonard Wood, Mo, listening on a radio. There was a strong thunderstorm raging and it was very difficult to hear. This makes no sense. What station would have carried a Pirate-Brave game in central Missouri? Did I really hear this game? Or was I listening to KMOX St. Louis and the Cardinals and they were just giving updates? There was a radio connection of some kind. The second of the two impossible games is even closer to home, and I was there.

I had the privilege of coaching baseball at Logan from 1971 to 1975. We went to the State Tournament three of those years, losing in the quarter finals in 1974 and the semi-finals in 1975. If ever you doubt the impact of having solid coaching in fundamentals, consider these players I had. All of our players were savvy baserunners, for example. One day it occurred to me that I had never taught them how to slide. Didn't have to. They came through the Boys Club program (girls were added later). In those days the Boys Club was a Northside venture. Terry Erickson and his staff taught the basic skills of the game and they played all summer. Jay Buckley would eventually do the same with his Juniors program on the Southside. Aquinas had a summer team, the A's. Baseball is a game of repetition. Buckley invented the five-inning doubleheader. All of this is appropriate for an area with a rich baseball background. It produced sound baseball players, and Frank Thornton, Dave Bruha, and I benefitted from those programs.

There was another factor in our success. We had some talented baseball players. Many high school coaches struggle with the catching position. There are so many dimensions and requirements associated with catching. It's hard to find one. We had two catchers. Both of them made the All City Team in 1975, Jim Loken and Rick Jorgenson. They split the time pretty evenly, playing right field when not catching, and they never complained about not playing their favorite position. The 1974 and 1975 teams were made up of good players; I'm not going to name any more for fear of overlooking someone, but there were two stars in this galaxy that were a little easier to see.

 Jeff Marson had an exceptional arm. A baseball game can be dominated by a pitcher, and with Jeff on the mound our probability of winning was very high. He was a lefty with a lively fast ball, an effective breaking pitch, and wonderful control, especially for a lefty. He was drafted by the Oakland A's, but chose to play Junior College ball first. Eventually he hurt his arm, an all-too familiar story. Guffy Twite was the other standout. His Dad Ralph played for the 1949 Logan team that lost in the State Championship finals. I never saw a high school shortstop with a better arm and with that tool he could be effective as a pitcher. Wisconsin recruited him to play shortstop, and soon they would drop baseball. I understood why they dropped boxing. I didn't understand, or forgive, them for eliminating baseball.

Jeff Marson, ace lefthander for the Rangers.

1973 City Champions, the Logan Rangers

THAT'S MY BOY — La Crosse Logan baseball coach Bill Leonard gives his catcher, Jim Loken, a hand and shout of joy following Loken's bases-loaded triple in the eighth inning which sparked the Rangers to an 8-2 victory over La Crosse Central in regional tournament baseball Tuesday. The win gives Logan a 14-2 record.

**A happy moment with Jim Loken,
who left us too early.**

It was the 1971 team, though, that played the impossible game. I'm trying to avoid using the Cinderella cliché, but I don't think I can. Cinderella's step sisters had luxurious gowns; she had a shabby dress. Our 1971 team smelled of moth balls. Not only were the uniforms old and worn, there were barely enough to go around. I pieced together my own uniform from stuff I had in a cedar chest at home. We entered tournament play well on the losing side of the ledger. Aquinas and Central shared the City Championship; we lost to both of them twice. Even after we made it to the State Tournament, the Tribune didn't send anyone to cover it. The bigger story the day before the tournament opened was the hiring of a new football coach at Central. Call it in, Coach.

But we were not without merit. We had two pitchers, real pitchers, Pete Kohnert and Ken Happel. They were not good enough to have scouts following them, but they were solid. Our shortstop Gordie Rieber, from a baseball family, hit .350 and gave our infield stability. The old baseball saying is that you have to be good up the middle. We were. Bob Kaiser was a good catcher who could hit. Jeff Stuhr in center was the best athlete on the team, though football was his best sport. He had speed, a good arm, and he hit over .300. Our corners, however, ended up being the story.

Brian Brose at first and Mike Pfennig at third were both seniors and both playing their first year of high school baseball. They had run track for three years. I didn't recruit them and I never asked them about their motivation to play baseball. The other two starters were Vince Hogden, who had a big homerun on the tournament trail, and Pete Weber, just a sophomore who could fill in at several positions as we shuffled our pitchers.

Maybe we should have seen something special coming after our first tournament game with Central, who had beaten us twice during the regular season and who led us 3-0 as we came to bat in the top of the seventh and last inning. This had been a pitcher's battle, our Ken Happel against Bobby Reichgelt. The game had been scoreless until the bottom of the fifth When Dan Hole hit a two-run homerun and suddenly it looked as though this game was going to form.

Bob Kaiser started our half of the seventh with an infield single. It's always good to have a catcher who can run. Pfennig walked and Hogden struck out. Brian Brose, former sprinter, beat out an infield hit to load the bases. Pete Weber hit a sharp single to drive in a run and keep the bases loaded. Happel was hit by a pitch to force in the second run. Central brought in a reliever and Gordy Rieber, after falling behind 0-2, worked him for a walk to force in a run to tie the game. Jeff Stuhr put down a perfect suicide squeeze to plate Weber with the go-ahead run. Logan 4, Central 3 and we go to the bottom of the seventh. Kenny Happel, whose final pitching line would be three runs, eight hits, three walks and no strikeouts, retired Central on three straight pop ups. This wasn't the impossible game, but it was the improbable.

Brevity is the soul of wit. I just made that up. Let's condense what happened leading to the impossible game. Kohnert throws two no hitters. We beat an undefeated Westby pitcher whose team was 13-1. Gordy Rieber has three hits in another game;

Bob Kaiser chips in with a stand up triple. In a key game against the South Central champions Sauk Prairie, Vince Hogden hits a grand slam into the trees beyond left field at Sauk City. Happel gets another key pitching win and he, Pfennig, and Brose all have two hits in a game. Jeff Stuhr has a three-hit game in there, and Happel pitches out of a bases-loaded, no outs inning. We are going to the State Tournament and in the words of sports writer Jim Pickett " This team never figured to go anywhere." I think he meant it as a compliment.

The little town of Marion in central Wisconsin poured tens of thousands of dollars into their ball park, plus a lot of sweat equity, and won their bid to host the State Tournament. First up was Chetek who had beaten Superior to get there, and Kohnert shut them down 8-0, setting the stage for the impossible game against Beloit. We will go right to the heart of the matter. We are coming to bat in the bottom of the seventh, and last, inning and trailing 8-3. But wait, it's darker than that. Scheduled hitters are the seventh, eighth, and ninth hitters. This is Casey redux. And then Beloit makes a crucial mistake.

Baseball people are infamous for their superstitions. Always (or never) step on the foul line on the way off (or on) the field. Don't say anything about the no hitter your pitcher has going; let him sit there at the end of the dugout by himself. Wear the same undershirt until you lose. My own, never let baseball shoes sit on the floor or in a locker or anywhere except in the correct left-right orientation. Beloit violated the biggest whammy of all. As I took up my station in the third base coaching box, I looked into their dugout. The bat bag was packed and it and the first aid kit were neatly stacked, along with the ball bag, helmets and all of their equipment. After all, this game was over. I don't know who was responsible for that, but guilt hangs heavily over them.

Brian Brose, who, upon further review, seemed to be in the middle of a lot of things on this journey, walked. Pete Weber was next, one of the youngest kids on this team. He had played well all year, and on top of that, he was one of my favorite kids. Yes, coaches have favorites, and if they tell you they don't, they are telling you a lie. I've got another sophomore on the bench, Tom Tischer, and I elect to have him pinch hit for Weber. He walks. After the game, I told Tom that I was awfully glad that he saw the take sign. Certainly we are going to take a strike in this situation. Tom's response; "I didn't see any take sign. I was too scared to swing." That was the end of Tom's career by the way. Next spring he decided he loved fishing a lot more than baseball and didn't come out. Happel singles and loads the bases. We need a bunch of runs so the base running is conservative. Beloit brings their closer in.

Rieber hits a sharp ground ball into the hole and the shortstop makes the only play he has, to third, except he throws it away and two runs score. Jeff Stuhr flies out to center and drives in a run in the process. Suddenly the score is 8-6. I wonder if the baseball gods would have been appeased if Beloit had unpacked their luggage at that point. They didn't. Kohnert grounds out to first for the second out. Bob Kaiser walks. Mike Pfennig then drives a ball all the way to the base of the wall in right center, a triple that drives in two runs and ties the score. The Red Sea has almost parted. Vince Hogden walks, bringing up Brian Brose for the second time in the inning. We are near the bottom of the order again. Brian hits a chopper deep up the middle. With two outs, our base runners can go at the crack of the bat. The shortstop makes a nice play, but with Brian's speed there is no way he can get him. He's safe on a close but uncontested play. Pfennig scores from third. Game over.

The State Championship game the next day was anti climatic. The old pro Pete Kohnert gave Chippewa Falls ten hits but he was masterful when he had to be, leaving twelve Chippewa runners on base, striking out eight and walking only one. Happel, Stuhr, Kohnert, Kaiser and Weber all had a hit, and Vince Hogden had two. There was a great caravan back to town and a large crowd gathered on the east steps of the old Logan High School building for a joyous celebration. Bobby Reighelt, a pitcher for Central, was in the crowd and the paper quoted him as saying "It should have been us". It wasn't a mean statement. Give him credit for being there. By all laws of the universe, he was probably right.

FLASHING NO-HIT FORM—La Crosse Logan's Pete Kohnert flashes the form which gave him a no-hit, 10-0 victory over Cashton in the subregional finals at Cashton Friday. Tribune Photo by Steve Noffke

Pete Kohnert, a key to our State Championship team.
He and Ken Happel were a one-two punch.

Chapter 10

Nice Guys Don't Finish Last

In modern times, roughly defined as the last 50 years, the native area player who has made the most impact in major league baseball is the West Salem native Damian Miller. Jerry Augustine and Craig Kusick, because they played for UWL, might figure in the voting, though neither is a native to the area. A case could be made for Scott Servais who, like Miller, had an eleven-year major league career and a reputation as an excellent defensive catcher and handler of pitchers. Beyond his playing days, Servais remains active in the front office of the Angels and his story is told in an earlier chapter. An aside, at one time there were three Coulee Region catchers on major league rosters at the same time, the third being George Williams, a former Central High School player, whose four-year career was cut short by injury.

His lifetime batting average was .243, but in 1997 he hit .289 in 76 games for Oakland, not an insignificant achievement.

Miller is the "Nice Guy" of the chapter title: self-effacing, humble, generous, husband, father, youth coach. He is what most fans would appreciate in any professional athlete, a good citizen. He is not without numbers and achievements. He has a World Series ring from the 2002 Series with Arizona, where he caught Randy Johnson, this year voted to the Hall of Fame in his first year of eligibility, and Curt Schilling who will someday be in the Hall. They were both twenty-game winners that year. Damian had two doubles and a key RBI in the All Star game that year, a year marred by the emergence of steroids, a labor dispute over revenue sharing, and the death of Ted Williams. He might have been the All Star Game MVP had one been chosen. This was the game, at Miller Park in Milwaukee, that ended in a tie after 11 innings. Both teams ran out of pitchers and the game was called. No MVP was chosen, though Joe Buck and Tim McCarver of the media suggested it be Miller.

Damian was drafted by the Twins in the 1990 draft and persevered in the lower reaches of professional baseball until he made his major league debut in 1997. His last game was September 30th of 2007, when he retired at age 37. He had offers from several major league teams who were in need of backup catchers with his documented numbers and his experience, but he chose to call it a career. As he put it, "I had enough room service meals." He had a lifetime batting average of .262 with 87 home runs and 406 RBI's. In 1998 he hit .286 with Arizona and in 2004, his single year with Oakland, he hit .272 with 9 home runs as the regular catcher, appearing in 110 games. In the grand scheme of things, the World Series and the All Star experiences were foremost career accomplishments, but he, and those of us present for it, surely value the walk-off three-run home run he hit to beat Cincinnati in a La Crosse Day game at Miller Park, a game that Geoff Jenkins, the Brewer outfielder, thought all of La Crosse was seated behind him in right field. More interesting than the numbers, which you can find if you have a mouse, were some of Damian's stories, shared with me over breakfast at Features.

The topics came in no particular order, one story suggesting another. I asked about doctored baseballs and Damian said that he never caught anyone who did that, but Todd Stottlemeyer, whom he did catch, was proficient in using a scuffed ball. The secret was in the grip and the placement of fingers and it made the pitch more lively and therefore more difficult to hit. In today's major league game if the ball touches the ground, it is thrown out of play. During much of Damian's career, that was not the case, and a ball that hit the dirt hard might be back in play, much to Todd Stottlemeyer's delight, and some other pitchers as well.

Stottlemeyer's name suggested the next thread of a story as well. He was pitching to Charley Hayes, and for some perhaps forgotten reason there was bad blood between the two of them for starters. Hayes doubles. Words are exchanged. As Damian put it, " suddenly I'm at the mound trying to save my pitcher, but I have no idea what happened because I'm at the bottom of the pile." One day Bobby Bonds was going wild because a pitch hit him. Damian tried to tell Bonds that it was a breaking ball. If the pitcher had tried to hit him it wouldn't be with a curve. Damian added " this happened when Bonds was my size" an obvious reference to Bonds' blowing up after steroid use.

A question you would have wanted to ask had you been there would have been "Who was the toughest pitcher you faced, the guy you least liked to go up against?" The answer was Kevin Brown of the Padres, a 6-6 giant of a man whose fastball was in the 94-97mph range. Though not in the Hall, Brown struck out 2,397 batters in a nineteen-year career. He walked 901, just wild enough, I would think to give pause. Dr. Mike Haupert of UWL, an economist who specializes in the salaries of professional athletes, could tell us that Brown's salary over the last six years of his career was $15 million dollars each year. The average major league salary today is $3.5 million, and the minimum is $600k.

Damian had some Randy Johnson stories, and I have one. I was visiting the Louisville Slugger bat factory one day. You can stand at the plate, fully protected from anything hitting you, and dial up a pitcher from a menu. I chose Johnson, the Big Unit. His image winds up 60 feet and 6 inches away and you see legs and arms and the pitch arrives. Suddenly. Frightening. Damian caught the game in which Johnson struck out 20 batters. He, Damian, was away doing an interview, and when he got to his locker, he found the lineup card with the 20k's on it and Randy's signature, his way of saying "thanks".

Every pitcher has a guy who "owns" him, a batter who is a tough out. For Johnson it was Marcus Giles of the Atlanta Braves. Giles had a seven-year career and a .277 batting average over that span, with a peak of .316 in 2003. His brother Brian had a longer career with better numbers. Randy Johnson, according to Damian, had two pitches, a 96 to 100mph fastball and a 92mph slider. For some reason, Johnson wanted to throw a splitter and he worked on it between starts, finally suggesting that Damian find a situation to call for it. So let Damian tell the story. "One day we had a good count on Giles, and I put the sign down for the splitter. Giles laced a screaming line drive to the gap that Steve Finley barely ran down for the third out. On the way to the dugout Johnson scowled at me and barked ' no more of that bleep', as though it were my idea." You wouldn't want to get hit by a pitch from Randy Johnson, and Walt Weiss didn't either. Weiss was a decent hitter and someone, oddly, who was dabbling in mixed martial arts on the side. He was a true tough guy and he got hit by a Johnson pitch. "You and me outside after the game" barked Weiss. This wasn't going to be one of those baseball fights, deep into restraint. After the game, the phone rang and the clubhouse man came to Johnson "It's for you." Johnson didn't take the call. Was it Weiss on the other end of the line, or someone pimping Johnson? We'll never know.

A person who had a great influence on Damian's career was Phil Roof, his manager in both Double A and Triple A. Roof had been a catcher and he stressed that the position was more than hitting and throwing people out at second base. It's managing the game. Knowing the hitters. Meeting every need. For starting pitchers, every five days the world stops for them. It's meetings and scouting reports and planning.

Damian had told me long ago that the major league catcher calls the pitches. That's not what he looks into the dugout to see. It has to do with the baserunner. The manager might ask for a sign telling the pitcher to use a slide step on the next pitch so that the delivery is quicker, making a steal that much more difficult. It might ask for a throw over, or a step off, or a "hold" where the pitcher comes set and stays there, hoping to get an indication of what the batter is going to do. Or the delay might just tighten up the hitter a bit. Miller also spoke highly of Tom Kelly, his manager with the Twins. Kelly loved "grinders", guys like Damian Miller who were not super stars but who worked hard at their craft. One day in a spring training game Brian Harper the catcher was on base when the inning ended, so Damian put on a mask and ran out to take the pitcher's warmup throws. When Harper appeared, Damian walked back to the dugout. Tom Kelly put his arm around Damian's shoulder and said " Son, we run out and we run back." Damian said, after that he always did.

One of Damian's career highlights, already alluded to, was the 2002 All Star Game. Mike Piazza of the Mets started for the Nationals, and Damian caught the middle innings, nearly becoming the MVP in the process. Benito Santiago of the Pirates finished. If you have watched any baseball from the period, you can see Santiago nearly spread-eagled behind the plate, looking like a limbo performer. His arm was so strong he could throw out runners from his crouch. One day against Pittsburgh Damian was up with a runner at first who tried to steal. Santiago with that cannon gunned him down. He looked up at Damian in the batter's box and with a calypso lilt that you can hear said "Mee'lar, thas why I drive a Mercedes". Later in the same game, he said to Damian, about the pitcher he was catching, " Not two Sundays in the big leagues and he is shaking me off".

We've all seen conferences on the mound where the pitcher is talking behind his glove so that no one can read his lips. Well, now we know what was said, at least once. A Brewer pitcher who shall remain unnamed said to Damian when facing a particularly good hitter in a tough situation " I have nothing to get this guy out with." The pitching coach had already departed the scene, I'm sure.

It has only been in the last decade or so that we hear baseball people talking about the "cutter". It's a short slider, determined by the grip. It is an effective pitch because it looks like a four-seam fastball, but it breaks like a slider, only not as much. Thus it can be thrown harder that a full-blooded slider. Mariano Rivera, said Damian, basically threw one pitch: a cutter. Another Miller comment, and he was quoting his close friend Craig Counsell " Anyone who could throw the ball 95mph was a freak. Now every single closer out of the bullpen throws 95mph or more." Damian has the highest regard for Robin Yount, who was a generation before him as a player but with whom he was associated when Yount was a bench coach both at Arizona and Milwaukee. First, he was humble. Speaking once of his 3,000 hits he said "It wasn't a big deal. I played twenty years and I never got hurt." It was a big deal, and so thought the Hall of Fame voters. Yount was described by many players as " the best teammate I ever had."

How about collisions at the plate, especially before the rule change limiting them somewhat? Miller had one that stands out in his memory, and it was with Adam Dunn. If you are a fan, you can picture this mountain of a man. The impending collision was bad because the throw was from the right side, giving the catcher no opportunity to see what is coming. I can attest to that. Geoff Jenkins hit the cutoff man who threw a perfect strike to Damian, who was launched quite a few feet. He held onto the ball. Dunn was out. No one was hurt.

Damian Miller, World Series and All Star catcher, and it started when Ed Servais suggested that Damian come to Viterbo where Servais was starting the baseball program, living proof that nice guys don't finish last.

Damian Miller Family

Damian is greeted after his walk-off homerun on La Crosse Day.

Chapter 11

The Lumber Yard

Love stories often begin with a chance encounter, a casual introduction, a meeting of eyes across the room, some seemingly insignificant event. Thus the Loggers were conceived. Ben Kapanke, son of Ruth and Dan, poured his heart into the Jim Evans Umpire School, along with another hundred hopefuls in his class. The top one-third of the group would be hired by professional baseball and would begin clawing their way toward the major leagues, an appointment that very, very few of them would reach. The attrition rate would be even greater than that of minor league players aiming for the top of the game. Ben Kapanke didn't make the cut.

He did, however, do better than average and that next stratum, that level of umpires-to-be that just missed the cut, would be offered spots in the several wood-bat summer college leagues. Ben caught on with the Northwoods League, referred to as the NWL from here on out. Being the good parents they are, Dan and Ruth Kapanke hit the road to watch Ben work, and Rochester was the closest NWL franchise. According to Dan, " Ben never missed a call." At least not while Ruth and Dan were present. At least not in their eyes.

And here comes the chance encounter, the spark that lit a fire. Mom and Dad were visiting with Ben after a Rochester Honker game, another flawless performance by Ben. Perhaps they were under the stands or in or near the umpires' room, some out-of-the-way place. They encountered not only Ben but also the head of the league, one Dick Radatz. Always the salesman and politician, Dan introduced himself and before long gave Radatz a throw-away line: "Have you ever considered La Crosse for a NWL franchise?" Well, yes he had. Had been looking at La Crosse for some time, in fact. A meeting was arranged. As with many love stories, the " what ifs " abound. What if the Kapankes hadn't chosen that game to attend? What if the league head had been at some other game, some other site that day? What if Radatz had been tied up with someone in another area of the park? What if Dan Kapanke had not initiated the contact? Ah, but they are playing our song.

The next step in this courtship was for Dick

Radatz to visit the Kapankes in La Crosse. This was like the boyfriend or girlfriend coming home to meet the parents. It doesn't seal the deal but it does suggest a high level of mutual interest. There are girls one dates and there are girls one brings home. They are different. Yes, we've tortured this metaphor enough, but Dan Kapanke wanted to make a good impression. Dan's real-life job was that of a seed salesman, dealing with farmers, a class of people he admired and deeply liked, and from which he came. His customers would often join him in his truck, straight from the hog barn or feed lot. That was what you smelled in his truck. It is a scientific fact that the olfactory nerves, our sense of smell, fatigue fairly quickly. Get enough of it and pretty soon you don't smell it. Radatz would smell it, though. So Dan borrowed Ruth's car for the meeting. There is another courtship analogy here, but I promised not to go there again.

 Lunch was at Fayzee's, a place we will always...stop that! Now they would tour the city to view the several ballparks and Radatz offered to drive. That was ok with Dan since Ruth's car, while it smelled nice, was not otherwise impressive. As they left Fayzee's and walked down the slight incline that is Pearl Street, they approached a Cadillac Escalade, and Dan slowed down and was about to approach the front passenger door, when he noticed that Dick Radatz was still walking. The league impresario stopped at a rusted-out Taurus with clothes hanging in the back, his wardrobe as he drove from franchise to far-flung franchise.

    At some point, perhaps after surveying Copeland Park, Radatz suggested that somehow they would need to assess what the City of La Crosse thought of all this, and the Mayor might be a good place to start. How much did Radatz know about the blood-letting that had occurred just ten years earlier? Would this be the same merry-go-round with a different horse? I shamelessly stole that line from Linda Heisler, a savvy La Crosse Alderperson of the time who led the opposition in shooting down a stadium then. It probably wasn't original with her, either.
At that time minor league professional baseball wanted to locate here, but we needed a ballpark. Mayor Pat Zielke was the force behind the move to get one built, and he appointed Steve Pavela to head the Baseball Committee, an excellent choice because Steve knew baseball and because his integrity was equal to eleven of the twelve Apostles. I am taking credit for that one. Ultimately the Committee secured pledges of $2.5 million, a huge share of that a gift from Sandy Gordon. The Chamber of Commerce endorsed the proposal; Sandy Hook, of memory, wrote an editorial supporting the effort and accompanied it with a $25,000 promise from the Tribune. The paper eventually listed all the potential donors and their amounts from Sandy Gordon's $1.5 million, through $100,000 each from several sources, right down to $5 pledges. The park was to be built on Copeland West, these days sometimes referred to as

Freedom Park, the boat landing area with the army tank along Clinton Street beyond the Black River. Even with donations of that magnitude, there would be some public money involved and so there was a referendum in November of 1989. The stadium was beaten badly, three to two. Game over. Mayor Zielke tried another fruitless tack, leading to the Heisler merry-go-round line. This establishes where we are in this narrative as Dick Radatz and Dan Kapanke bounce around town in the rusty Taurus. How, Radatz asked, could we arrange a meeting with the Mayor, John Medinger?

Unless you slept through several years either side of 1990, you know that the City of La Crosse and the Town of Campbell, the Republic of French Island as it is sometimes known and Kapanke's precinct, were embroiled in bitter and costly legal battles over annexation and water. But I repeat myself. Those two issues were often one. It is really high praise for both men to say that they had respect for each other and kept personal lines of communication open. So, to the Radatz question. Can we talk to the Mayor? There were no cell phones in those days but Radatz, whose car was his office and his closet, had one of those big mobile phones in the front seat. Kapanke punched the Mayor's direct line numbers by heart and it was immediately "Hi, John. This is Dan." That was followed shortly by, on the other end, " Come on up". Later Radatz would say that he knew that Kapanke was the right person for the franchise because he was connected.

Things moved pretty fast from there. It would cost about $360,000 to bring Copeland to minimum NWL standards. The Corrine Zielke fund granted $300,000 of that and the league loaned the Kapankes the remaining $60,000. The Common Council approved an original ten-year lease (since extended) and the rush was on to rehabilitate the park. From that point, and each year, improvements have been made as the Loggers flourished and sponsors stepped forward. Prior to this past season Barb and Dave Skogen and Festival Foods came forward with a major gift of $320,000 to install artificial turf in the infield. Not only does the turf provide true bounces with minimal upkeep, but it is under-laid with a drainage system that means that once the rain stops, the infield is immediately playable, The La Crosse Community Foundation has provided financial support. In turn, the park remains city property and is used by, in addition to the Loggers, Central, Western Technical College, the American Legion baseball program, and youth baseball teams. And, the Loggers have committed to support UWL baseball to the tune of $40,000 annually. The Eagles also play at Copeland.

The Loggers have been a success story and the Kapankes have spearheaded this effort, particularly impressive in the light of what might be described as local powers who are cautious and move slowly. The Loggers set an NWL attendance record for a first-year franchise, opening the gates to 86,991 fans in that first year of 2003. They went over the 100,000 mark the second year. The won-lost record went from 27-36 in the inaugural season to 34-32 the second year. The high water mark so far was the 2012 season when Field Manager Andy Mckay led the Loggers to a 53-21 record and the league championship, the second best mark in NWL history.

We can't forget Chris Goodell. He has been a huge factor in the Logger's success. Probably many fans overlook the hats this man wears: procurement, baseball equipment, merchandise, transportation and much more; marketing, season tickets, advertising in multiple media; player procurement and the important matter of relationships with college coaches all around the country; relationships with the league and other franchises; overall public relations. I should not have started this list because I don't know enough to give full credit. Be assured, it is more than a fulltime job, year-round. He was the NWL Executive of the Year twice and has been the La Crosse Tribune's Sports Person of the Year. And a possible source of a trivia question: as a mere boy he played baseball here on an Iowa team in the Stars of Tomorrow tournaments. I thought I read somewhere that he is a University of Dubuque graduate. If that is true, all of this is high praise from a Loras man.

Baseball-loving communities, and we are one, take pride in major league players who have played on their diamonds. In Eau Claire, for example, and we are talking here about organized, professional baseball, and an era long before the NWL scene, the locals there recall players who called Carson Park one of their minor league homes: Henry Aaron, Wes Covington, Andy Pafko, Billy Bruton, Bob Trowbridge, and Harry Hannebrink, among others. As we explained earlier, the NWL is not a professional league; it is, though, highly regarded as a launching pad for professional players. To date, eight major league players have honed their skills at the Lumber Yard. In the forefront of this list is Max Scherzer, a 2004 Logger, who recently signed a seven-year $210 million dollar contract to pitch for the Washington Nationals. It will take an army of actuaries to figure out all the permutations of his salary, portions of it deferred all the way out to 2028. This is roughly the Gross National Product of Elbonia. It is also why I would not buy an $8 beer at a major league park. My friend Don Salyards, an economist at Winona State University, would probably be horrified by the number, but I haven't checked with him so I am not going to put words in his mouth. But he would say something like this. "At least it's market-driven. If you can fan 11.1 major league hitters every nine innings, they will pay you that kind of dough." I would add that it doesn't matter your political affiliation, sexual orientation, color, vegan eating habits, or nation of origin. Don might not say that latter part because he is an economist, one of those people who make accountants look exciting.

The next former Logger is also a pitcher, Chris Sale, signed by the White Sox. He pitched in relief for the Sox in 2010 and 2011 and then became exclusively a starter. To date, he has put together a 40-26 record, and even more impressively, a career 2.76 ERA. (Scherzer, who won the Cy Young in 2013, has an ERA of 3.58).

Vic Black, Loggers 2007, has been called by the New York press a "lockdown reliever" for his work with the Mets. He pitches exclusively out of the pen and has a two-year ERA of 2.96, and strikes out more than twice as many people as he walks. He learned how to grind with the Loggers.

Jordan Pacheo, a 2005 Logger, has made an impact with the Colorado Rockies. In 2012, his best professional year thus far, hit .309 with five home runs in 475 at bats. Look for him this year, 2015, with the Diamondbacks; they picked him up on waivers from the Rockies. Don't worry about meal money; his 2014 salary was listed at $502,000.

We saw Danny Herrera pitch here in 2005. It appears that his professional career may be over, at least it looks that way based on available data. Danny was an interesting player because he was five feet- six inches tall and weighed 165 pounds with rocks in his pocket. It's a feel-good story though. In four years he pitched 131 major league innings, mostly with Cincinnati.

Brett Jackson, a Logger teammate of Vic Black in

2007, was signed by the Cubs after being drafted in 2009. He has appeared in 44 big league games with Chicago. He was traded to Arizona and had some playing time with them. His two years of service in the bigs to date add up to a .268 batting average with some power. He has the tools and some good years ahead of him. Obviously the San Francisco Giants think so too, since they picked him up in the 2014 Rule 5 draft. The World Champion Giants had a hole in their outfield, evidenced by Travis Ishikawa's defensive misadventures in the post season. He was a first baseman pressed into service in the outfield. The hill in San Francisco just got a little steeper for Jackson because just days ago the Giants signed Nori Aoki, he of the Brewers and Royals. Jackson, though, has realized part of his dream, and if the baseball gods are good to him, there is still more ahead.

Eric Thames was a Logger in 2007, a mid and post season All Star. He made his major league debut in 2011 when he played in 95 games for Toronto, batting .262 and hitting 12 home runs. He played with both Toronto and Seattle in 2012. He didn't play in the majors in 2013, spending time in AAA. He has been in the Baltimore organization, was claimed and then released by Houston. He dominated in the Korean major league in 2014, hitting .341 with 32 home runs and 113 RBIs. It will be interesting to see what 2015 brings to Eric Thames.

Finally, Rob Brantly, a catcher for the 2009 Loggers was drafted in the third round and signed by

BASEBALL, A LOVE STORY

the Tigers in 2010. He was traded to Miami in 2012. When one realizes how many already professional players are involved in various waivers and signings, one can see the value of the work of the professional scout like Mark Servais. Brantly hit .235 with four home runs over parts of two seasons with the Marlins. We will have to look for this former Logger catcher with the good baseball genes in the White Sox organization, since they selected him off waivers in December of 2014.

So we have seen right here in the Lumber Yard players who have made the majors. We will see more. In perspective, what can we expect? Based on a pretty good sample size, maybe 5% to 10% of a roster making it to the show? Add at least another 10% making it to the high minors. Better than that, though, almost all of the Loggers have improved their college game significantly here. They have learned hard work and discipline, a very few the hard way. They either opted out or were invited out. That number is miniscule because of Chris Goodell's connections and screening. In the meanwhile, local fans see high quality baseball and reasonable entertainment. Civic pride is part of the deal.

This love story has defied all odds. It could have been shot down by nay sayers who said we tried something like that ten years ago. Won't work. Move City Hall to try to accomplish this? Good luck. Fan support will fade quickly. Hardly. Where will you find supporters and sponsors with that kind of money?

The organization did. But here is where it really might have failed.

Dan Kapanke played farm field baseball whenever he could. He had parents who let him skip school to listen to the World Series on the radio when all the Series games were day games. He loved the game. He and Ruth (Bissen) were schoolmates at Luther High, in the early days of that institution when enrollments were small. Athletes in the spring could participate in two sports at the same time. Dan ran track and played baseball. The baseball coach was Herb Grams, a man both Dan and Ruth idolized. At the end of one spring, midway through Dan's high school years, Coach Grams put an arm around Dan's shoulder and said " Dan, next year I think you should concentrate on track."

It would have broken a lesser man's heart.

Chapter 12

On The Road Again

The miles across the isolated forest land clicked by rhythmically over the pavement expansion joints. The night was clear and cold. Inside the Winnebago motor home it was comfortably warm, conducive to sleep for anyone who had been exposed to the elements all afternoon. Most of the college football officiating crew that had worked a game that day at Northern Michigan were asleep in the several bunks or on the couches in the back. And why not. Friday night, after officiating with their respective high school crews, they had started out at midnight from La Crosse, heading to Marquette, Michigan, across several geophysical landforms and into the Eastern Time Zone. No one had been tired enough to easily fall asleep then, but that changed this Saturday night. Breakfast had been pancakes that Saturday morning at a diner in Marquette, followed by a shower and a stretching walk in the fresh air. Several had napped on mats in a gym. All of this was nearly 40 years ago. They approach officiating assignments at this level differently today. The first quarter of the game had been played in sunshine; the second, in a snow squall; the third in sunshine; the fourth in blowing lake flurries. Welcome to the Upper Peninsula.

Now they were on their way home. Jay Buckley was at the controls, smoothly guiding the rig at a steady five miles-per-hour below the speed limit. I was riding shotgun, responsible for calling out any wildlife that might be on or about to cross the road. I saw none. It was a peaceful, mellow time given to good conversation with an occasional snore from the back.

Jay has always been an epicure, a connoisseur, a traveler. He and I have a number of mutual interests: travel, history, cities, people, and – most importantly for this written work – baseball. We talked about all of those subjects, including where we had been and where we hoped to go someday. We probably underestimated how extensive that travel list would become.

You can't talk long about baseball in La Crosse without mentioning Jay. He was the assistant baseball coach at La Crosse Central for 29 years. Frank Thornton was the head coach for 30 years, putting together a 459-131-1 record. I was tempted just to drop that tie; it messes up the symmetry of the page, but there it is. Thornton had to get by without Buckley that first year, but for the next 29 they were great partners: Ferrante and Teicher, Stanley and Livingstone, Montgomery and Ward. Carson and McMahon, Thornton and Buckley. Together they achieved. They took teams to the State Baseball Tournament seventeen times, winning it twice and finishing second six times, a record matched by few if any. They were conference champions eighteen times, city champions 24. Frank Thornton was inducted into the State Baseball Coaches Association Hall of Fame in 1990; Buckley, in 2007, the only assistant coach to receive that honor. (Jack Nockles of Aquinas was inducted into the Football Coaches' Hall as an assistant and later became a head coach.).

Some of the success Central had was due to the Juniors program that Jay ran for underclassmen after school was out each summer. To be a good baseball player, some natural talent is required, but repetition is crucial. That's why Jay had the Juniors play every day in the summer, twice most days. That is why the Loggers start on-field work in the middle of the afternoon on their game days. The Juniors won all kinds of tournaments and honors, including a national 17 and under championship. You have to love the game to do what Jay did, and this is a love story. Jay would carve nearly a month out of the summer, the time between wrapping up the Juniors and the start of his school duties, to travel. He would load up the Thunderbird and head out, maybe to the East Coast or to New Orleans or to the Southwest. There was usually a plan but there was room for improvisation. What might be around the next bend, what historical site might be there, and if he chanced upon a baseball game, all the better. With hindsight, you can see Jay Buckley tours coming.

In about 1980 Jay, along with Jim Olson who owned the Alpine Inn, arranged a bus trip to see a baseball game. That made sense. Lots of bars did that. But a bigger idea was beginning to coalesce in Jay's mind. The next step was to put together a brochure, a handout, really, for Alpine patrons, promoting a multiple-day, multiple- park trip. That first tour was set for August of 1981. Three days before "D" Day, Major League baseball went on strike. The trip was scratched.

Not daunted, the pair brought off the first tour in 1982. After several years, Olson sold the Alpine and became a Ford dealer in Viroqua, and Jay was flying solo with the tour business. He had a good feel for who his customer base was going to be, and they were not a good fit for a tavern-based operation. Jay Buckley Baseball Tours really begins to come into focus. To borrow a term from the art world, the overview of the business would be a triptych: Vacation in the 70's; Hobby in the 80's; Fulltime business in the 90's. Jay left education and devoted his significant energies to the tour.

BASEBALL, A LOVE STORY

The Tour ran two trips in 1986. After a one-inch ad in the Sporting News, there were three trips in 1987. That ad generated responses from all over the country and what had been a local deal, suddenly took on a wider customer base. It grew from puppy love to the real thing. By 1990 Jay Buckley Baseball Tours ran fourteen trips. Today the number is around 30 per year. There have been challenges along the way. The 1994 baseball strike hurt the business for several years. And then there was the tour that featured the last game to be played in County Stadium. It fizzled with the tragic accident that killed several ironworkers in a crane collapse at the rising Miller Park, pushing the closing of the old park further into the next season. Jay was left with a ho-hum game between two teams going nowhere and just playing out the string at the end of the year. Cancellations poured in. The trip was scrubbed. Brighter things are associated with the tours.

Four marriages have been generated between people who met on the trip. One young man, who had been adopted, and who had for a long time been seeking his birth mother, got the final clue just before he left on the trip. His Mother was in Atlanta, a tour stop, and he met her there. One couple arranged their marriage a few blocks from Wrigley Field and got to the game for the first pitch. The groups are not perfectly gender-matched, but there are many good female fans on the trips. That's good. This is a love story.

The Jay Buckley baseball tour is the biggest and best of its kind. There are four competitors on the national scene now, in Boston, Charlotte, Indianapolis, and somewhere in Kentucky. Two of them are full-service, broad band travel companies for whom the baseball trips are a small part of what they do. At least one of the others is a high-end, luxury all the way operation with a price ticket to match. Four years ago Jay sold the business to Matt Thornton, Frank's son, but he remains active on the tours. Jay and Matt remain co-owners of a related memorabilia business.

In the middle of all this, Jay was a force in the local Stars of Tomorrow tournaments. If you were not around to observe the "Stars" phenomenon, you would find the spectacle hard to believe. It started with Cootch Carroll putting together a youth tournament for a handful of teams in the late 60's, paying the umpires and other expenses, such as kids returning foul balls, out of his sock. Literally. He had a long elastic sock where he kept his money and who knows what else. The tournament grew beyond what Cootch wanted to manage, and he passed the torch. At its peak there were 225 teams over several weeks, divided into age-related divisions, and again into "open" or all star teams, and teams that played together all year. Don Benden, Dave Bruha, Bob Maringer, Duke Coughlin, and Jay Buckley, among others, took leadership roles in this massive effort. Just as town team baseball faded, the "Stars" would eventually fade, but in their ascendancy, the tournament took over the city. The finals were aired on local radio, and I have a mental picture of Jess Ondell, sponsor of several Major Drugs teams, doing color radio work from the top row of the pre-Logger stands at Copeland.

Jay Buckley's resume, then, includes Hall of Fame high school coaching, major contributions of effort and leadership in one of the premier youth baseball tournaments in the nation, and the founding of a highly successful baseball tour business. That's a pretty good trifecta. And I have a first-hand report on one of the tours.

Years ago, my wife gave me a trip for my birthday. We started in La Crosse. Not all tours do. Some of them, especially the spring training ones, are "fly-ins" and the groups meet in Florida or Arizona. I saw the roster of my trip ahead of time and I knew that Jon Kozidowski and his son Mike, from Winona would be on this trip. I was prepared. We had played together a few times more than 50 years ago, but mostly we were in opposite dugouts. He quick-pitched me one night. Nasty deed. I was digging in and checking where the trademark was and a pitch zipped by. Startled me. Dangerous. I took a few threatening steps toward the mound, barking, but not so fast that the catcher and the umpire couldn't restrain me. We laughed about that on the bus, but we were not laughing when it happened. At least, I wasn't laughing.

One of the great things about a Buckley trip that I don't recall being advertised is that for maybe 1,600 miles you are with twenty or thirty other people who love baseball, and each one has his or her story. Natural selection at work. We saw the Cubs at Wrigley and visited the Louisville Slugger bat factory in that Kentucky city. It was on to Cincinnati, Detroit, Cleveland, and Toledo for a Mudhen AAA game, and back to Chicago and the White Sox park. We ran into Bert Blyleven in the concourse at Cleveland and I had my picture taken with him. Only later did I notice that he put the horns over my head. He was there to broadcast for the visiting Twins. If you love baseball, this is like a honeymoon.

CHUCK HOCKENBERY P

Chapter 13

The Comeback Kid

The 54-year-old man, trim and virile, was brushing his teeth in the morning when half his body, including vision and speech, stopped working. His thrashing around alerted his wife, who had a background in physical therapy, and knew immediately what was happening. She dialed 9-1-1. Her quick action and the EMTs saved his life. With a major stroke, the victim needs help quickly. At some point early on the doctors told the man that his vision would probably return, but it wasn't likely that he would be able to walk. It looked like the nursing home at best.

Those doctors probably didn't know that Chuck Hockenberry had been a competitor all his life. He had rattled around the fields and sandlots of Onalaska with older kids, playing uphill. He had looked up to the likes of Everett Johnson and Dave Skogen. He wanted to be like Barry Frietag. He horsed around with Tim and Tom Gullickson. In high school he ran the quarter mile and to do that well you have to be tough mentally and physically. It also helps if you don't mind throwing up. He was a state champion high jumper and he threw the shot. In those years Onalaska played high school baseball in the summer, so Chuck could do both sports. He was also a quarterback and safety on Roy Grade's football team. He wasn't an easy out, and he wasn't going out easily. The rehab from the stroke was the biggest physical challenge of his life. Today he walks purposefully around the track at the YMCA, looking like any other 64-year-old man striding along. There is just a very small sag to the right side of his mouth, but it actually looks like a puckish grin, a friendly look. He answered all my questions, evidencing the ability to both recall and communicate clearly. He is enjoying life. Chuck Hockenberry threw a lively fastball in high school. I saw it close up because I was the plate umpire for several games he pitched. Professional baseball people can teach young players a lot about the game; they can't teach you to throw hard. Oh, they can add a few miles per hour with improved mechanics and different arm slots and the use of the lower body, but that window of improvement is pretty small. You can throw hard or you can't. Chuck could. Maybe the first scout who took a close look at him was Dale McReynolds, a wonderful gentleman now deceased. He was a Cincinnati scout when I first met him; he ended up with the Dodgers. It was Ernie Rudolph of the Angels who really urged that franchise to sign Chuck.

Imagine this high school kid from Onalaska reporting to the Quad Cities not many weeks after graduation. I can tell you about his minor league career, especially the seven years leading to his major league debut in 1975, statistics and all that. I probably will, but I found the by- play around that journey, the human interest angles, the being called out of an afternoon movie in Albuquerque to pack his bags because the Angels had called him up, more interesting than the numbers. He was called out of the show to go to the show. Lovely. The minor league trail had been challenging, and, appropriate, I suppose, for a West Coast franchise: Quad Cities, Idaho Falls, Idaho, Bend, Oregon, El Paso, Texas, Stockton, California, Shreveport, Louisiana, and Salt Lake City, that last stop AAA in the Pacific Coast League. Lots of bus rides in the early years; meal money at $ 2.50. Chuck had an interesting perspective on Triple A, the last hurdle leading to the Majors. Pitching in Triple A was maybe more difficult than in the Majors. For one thing, some of the hitters there were not in the big time yet because their defense was inadequate, a liability the big club couldn't afford. So they hit the stuffing out of the ball while they learned the nuances of major league defense. These several leagues in the southwest had diamonds that got sun baked and hard, given to quick bounces and bad bounces. People got on base that wouldn't have on the manicured fields of the big time. And the Major League defense behind you in the big time bailed you out of maybe one jam a night, a break you didn't get in El Paso. The climb got tougher the higher you went.

One of Chuck's minor league teammates, a roommate in fact, was the movie star Kurt Russell. Not being a movie buff, I had to check on that. Kurt Russell, at 10 years old, was in an Elvis Presley movie "It Happened at the World's Fair". Walt Disney himself signed Russell to a ten-year contract. Russell wanted more than anything to be a Major League baseball player and he made movies in the off season. He ended up appearing in scores of films, many of them cult movies. One of the more famous was "Silkwood". He and Goldie Hawn have been partners for more than thirty years and have a son. They live on a ranch outside Aspen, the name of which is "Home Run Ranch". He hooked up with Hawn in 1984 when they both appeared in the movie "Swing Shift".

The bulk of Russell's baseball career was 1971 to 1973, three seasons, and his career batting average was a very respectable .292. In four or five games at the end of his baseball career, at the next highest level, he was hitting over .500 when he totally ruined a rotator cuff. His friend Ron Shelton wrote the Crash Davis role in "Bull Durham" with Russell in mind, but the studio insisted on Kevin Costner. One more human interest angle, if you are up for it. One of the bigger "names" that Chuck played with, both in the minors and then with the Angels, was a pitcher all hard core baseball fans would recognize immediately, Frank Tanana. He was a front line guy. When was the last time Chuck saw him? Probably that one shining half year with the Angels, 1975. They shared an apartment for a brief time. In the throes of Chuck's rehab, Frank Tanana called him to see how he was doing and to encourage him. Chuck has no idea how Frank found out.

Early in his career it became apparent that his role was going to be one of short relief and that challenging position may have contributed to Chuck's fighting spirit. Almost any time a short reliever comes in, there is trouble. Men on base. The game on the line. No way to be super careful with a hitter because the last thing the manager wants is yet another base runner. And the further up the food chain you go, that is, the more advanced the league, the tougher the hitters are. Make a mistake and they will hit it hard. I asked him about people. He played with Mickey Rivers and Wade Boggs in the minors. One of his pitching coaches was Johnny Sain. You may remember the couplet about the 1948 Boston Braves "Spahn and Sain and two days of rain", a withering comment on the overall quality of that pitching staff.

The overall record, Chuck Hockenberry's Major league line, isn't going to make him eligible for the Hall of Fame ballot: he was 0-5 with a 5.27 ERA. He appeared in 16 games, pitching 41 innings and had one save. That 1975 staff he was on had Frank Tanana 16-9, Ed Figueroa 16- 13, and Nolan Ryan 14-12. The Angels were 72-89, 6th in the American League west.

Chuck relieved Nolan Ryan at Yankee Stadium and remembers Thurman Munson as a particularly tough out. He made a start against the White Sox, facing off with Wilbur Wood, the knuckleballer. He struck out the side against Baltimore in a one-inning stint. The 1975 season was the end of the big time for Chuck. He played winter ball that year for Jose Pagan, a manager he really admired. He had a staph infection and had to come home early. He was the last cut at the end of the 1976 spring training, and ended up being released at the end of 1976. Oakland signed him a year later and he had some time with Jersey City in the Eastern League and Vancouver in the PCL, two places on this earth that couldn't be more different. All together, Chuck pitched in nine seasons of minor league baseball and ended up with a record of 42-42, and a 4.13 ERA, 782 innings of challenging baseball. This man was a warrior, one of a very few local men to appear in the big leagues. He earned respect everywhere he went. Those are the numbers. I have one more human interest angle.

Gene Autry, the singing cowboy, owned the

Angels. If I have to tell you who he is, this story won't matter anyway. One day at spring training Chuck and his friend and roommate Frank Tanana are walking through the hotel lobby in the training complex. Autry is sitting at the end of the bar and he motions the two of them in. Dick Williams, the manager, had declared the hotel bar off limits to the players. I'm sure he had no illusions about where else the players might refresh themselves, but it wasn't going to be the hotel bar. Chuck and Tanana told Autry they couldn't come in. Autry said "If I say you can, you can. Come on in." And one more Autry story. One year an Onalaska friend, Earl Cook, drove Chuck's car west for him. When they hooked up, Earl wasn't interested in the baseball players. He was a big Gene Autry fan and he was thrilled to get his autograph on a napkin.

So this is part of the love story of baseball. It's Chuck's wife taking care of him in the clutch, and making it possible for them to appreciate their grandchildren. It's Chuck's love for the game. And Chuck may not have realized this, but his story, his achievements, have brought to all of us who are baseball fans here in our part of the world, joy and pride. The Comeback Kid came back.

Chapter 14

The Men In Blue

    Where did they come from? Who were they? With fifty or more amateur teams in a several county area in the early 1950's, where did they find enough umpires? I can only name a few. Cootch Carroll and Pip Wuest were ubiquitous, usually working together, Cootch behind the plate and Pip on the bases. Still in high school but playing summer ball, I remember barking immaturely about a call. I don't remember exactly what Pip said to me but it amounted to " It doesn't make you look good. It doesn't help. And you shouldn't do it." It made a great impression on me. We would often encounter Horace Moran and Hugh Blank, though not necessarily working together. Tom Reindl of Westby popped up often. Maybe Ken Trott? I'm embarrassed that I don't remember more of these people, often the target of abuse, but without whom there would be no game. Cootch was one of a kind.

After our pitcher had his half-dozen warmup throws before the start of an inning, I'd look around to see Cootch back at the screen behind home plate in deep conversation with one or more fans, often different fans each inning. He was enjoying the chat and in no hurry to resume the game. Whether it was intentional or not, I think this dalliance with the patrons endeared Cootch to them and almost eliminated really ugly words that would otherwise be directed at him over contested calls. Complaints he received were generally good natured.

Cootch was a cultured man in his own unshaven way, and one with an expansive vocabulary. He was also one who would cut loose with some pretty colorful language when he caught a foul tip on the toe or any part of his body. He used an external chest protector, the balloon type. Old time fans will remember them. Eventually they disappeared. I always thought that the external protector, bulky thing that it was, caused the umpire to have trouble at the bottom of the strike zone. Cootch called a lot of low balls strikes, fine if you were in the field but not so good if you were batting. He was consistent. Because I spent so much time crouched in front of this man, we developed an almost symbiotic relationship, exchanging conversation, especially if the batter wasn't in the batter's box at the moment. One summer he campaigned to fix me up with his wife's younger sister. I'm sure she was a charming young person, but I was playing baseball 87 out of 90 days and nights that summer and wasn't paying much attention to my social calendar. About the third inning he would tell me about her good looks. By the sixth inning he would have moved on to her cooking and baking skills. " Cootch, I'm trying to manage the game for my pitcher, and, by the way, you are taking the corner away from us."

After my playing days, I umpired for some years, usually with Jim Knutson. We were both old catchers and we both enjoyed the plate, but we traded off evenly, plate and bases. We had several misadventures. We were working a two-day WIAA regional tournament at Arcadia. The second night I had the plate. In the second or third inning one of the middle infielders called time out and said to Jim " Hey ump, second base isn't where it was last night." Now, this is a fairly alarming statement, especially because, if it were true, it would have been a pretty serious oversight on our part. It was true.

Apparently Don Smith, the Arcadia coach and the tournament manager, whose team had been eliminated the night before, had his family and his camper packed up and they were gone on vacation. He had delegated- or not delegated – field preparation to someone. Did they put the bases in the wrong place? Or maybe there had been a pony league game that afternoon and the bases hadn't been changed. They were all 10 feet short of regulation. Ten feet!

Surely someone would have noticed that before the third inning. Maybe the umpires?

What to do now? Fortunately the score was tied. After we wiped the egg off our faces, we immediately had the bases put in their proper places and said "play on". It was a Solomon-like adjudication, but not one good enough for Jim Crowley the Arcadia Athletic Director. Pre-cell phone, he scrambled somewhere and tracked down someone at the WIAA. It was the 6th inning before he got back with their answer, which was exactly what we had done.

Another night at Gale-Ettrick, Jim had the plate. We were working for Pug Lund there, an excellent coach, always one of my favorite guys, though he could get in your face. There was a leather-lung fan with a deep, booming voice who was on Jim from the second pitch. It was relentless. It wasn't vulgar or profane but it was critical, loud, and annoying. You never obviously look to see who this is, but between innings Jim would come down around first base to visit as the team in the field took their warm ups. I was rather enjoying the spectacle but Jim was getting more and more steamed. We'd sneak a peek but we couldn't spot the fellow.

We were walking up the hill to the parking lot after the game and Jim had just said, quietly to me, teeth on edge, " I'd like to see that guy…" and almost on cue the voice boomed in our ears, from right behind us with one last blast of criticism. Jim wheeled around and there he was, a wizened up old man who had to have been 90. He could not have weighed more than 120 pounds. He was struggling up the hill behind his walker. Where he got that stentorian voice is a mystery. We laughed half the way home.

One last story about this dynamic umpiring duo. We were working an Onalaska high school game and I have the bases. Player or umpire, you just don't step on the field without your protective cup in place. Maybe I had to hurry from work and, because I knew I had the bases, I took a shortcut in suiting up. I didn't have a cup and let's just say I wasn't dressed to use one. It wasn't long before Jim took a wicked foul tip to the chest-neck-arm that really rocked him. It might have been Chuck Hockenberry firing a heater. You know how hard a baseball is and fouled off the edge of a bat from a few feet away it can have the force of a taser. After some recovery time, a still dazed Knutson said he could continue, but on the bases.

I got the inside chest protector on and adjusted the mask. We had long since stopped wearing shin guards. But that's all the protective equipment I had. You have seen caricatures of someone who has to go to the bathroom. Knees together, sort of hunched over. I was that figure. I got as close behind the catcher as the law would allow. I finished the game unscathed.

Warming up, I do remember another umpire now, although he worked high school games and later, including some of our games at Logan. John

Gilson had gone to umpire school, maybe the same Jim Evans School that Ben Kapanke had. He must have excelled at balk recognition. I don't think I ever saw him work a game that he didn't call a balk. To be fair, many high school balks aren't called. At the ground rule discussion pre-game I was always tempted to ask him to call the balk early so we could get it out of the way. I didn't ask; I thought I might get tossed for that. I had an interesting experience working basketball with John.

He and I were seldom basketball partners; in fact, this may have been the only time we worked basketball together. As the first half progressed, it seemed to me that John really called the game tight. What I thought was incidental contact, he called a foul. To me, it seemed to be impacting the flow of the game, and there were people on both teams in foul trouble (in itself, not a reason to not call a foul). I was mentally rehearsing a way to bring this to his attention tactfully at halftime. We got to our dressing room and before I could say anything I had carefully rehearsed, he said " My God, Bill, you are letting them get away with murder. You have to tighten up." I don't remember the second half.

In these later years there was, and is, an umpire who probably worked more games than anyone, even more than Cootch and Pip had in their time. John Gruden. He worked all levels: youth, high school, college, semi pro, town team, Legion. If they played around here, he umpired. He told me a baseball story

BASEBALL, A LOVE STORY

once that I have never forgotten. It's romantic in the classical sense in that it conveys feeling, emotion. It tugs a bit at the heart. We played college baseball against each other, he at Winona State and I at Loras. He was a good left-handed hitter. We are the same age which means we were both about nine at the end of World War II. We were located worlds apart at that time.

I can't recall all the details, but he was from Yugoslavia, a part of the world that has changed flags and boundaries multiple times. In the last stages of the war, John and his family were caught between the Nazi's and the Reds. Either side might have killed them. They hid under hay on a wagon to escape. It was touch and go but the family got to New York by boat. John's Father got a job on the Iron Range in Northern Minnesota.

Here is this nine-year old boy who speaks no English thrust into the classroom and onto the playground. The boys are playing baseball at recess and noon hour. John has no experience with the game, none. Kids can be cruel, but kids can also be kind. A classmate took John under his wing and showed him how to hold the bat and how to swing. The kid was a left-handed hitter. That is why John, whose dominant hand is right and who writes and eats and does everything else right-handed, hits from the left side of the plate. Because his friend was left-handed.

It's a great game.

Chapter 15

Baseball Legends

How great a game? Here is what W.P. Kinsella says.

"I don't have to tell you that the one constant through all the years has been baseball. America has been erased like a blackboard, only to be rebuilt and then erased again. But baseball has marked time with America, has rolled by like a procession of steamrollers. It is the same game that Moonlight Graham played in 1905. It is a living part of history, like calico dresses, stone crockery, and threshing crews eating at outdoor tables. It continually reminds us of what once was, like an Indian Head penny in a handful of new coins."

W.P. Kinsella
Shoeless Joe

BASEBALL, A LOVE STORY

In Kinsella's novel, some unseen public address announcer told the main character, also named Kinsella, "If you build it, he will come." It wasn't a bellowing, siren-like, drawn-out announcement like one hears at player introductions everywhere at every level these days, feeding the culture's need for decibels, for noise. Almost everywhere. The hated Yankees do it differently. Mellow. Sonorous. Flat. Solemn. Deep. "Batting third, Derek Jeter." More like announcing the entrance of deity. It's about the only thing I like about the Yankees. But the voice told Ray Kinsella to build the field.

Author Kinsella's book, made into the movie "Field of Dreams", is a fanciful tale. That is understatement. The protagonist turns part of his failing and highly-leveraged Iowa farm into a baseball field so that "He", Shoeless Joe Jackson and his disgraced 1919 Chicago White Sox teammates, can come back and play baseball again. They are ghosts who appear out of a cornfield. Only the true believers can see them.

If the lack of realism is a problem, you will have to ignore Ray Kinsella's plan to kidnap the reclusive writer J.D. Salinger and bring him back to Iowa to help with the project. Why Salinger? He is a real person (now deceased) and a baseball fan. He has a character named "Kinsella" in his most famous work "Catcher In The Rye".

That "Catcher" was not a baseball catcher. You

know that if you read the book. The writing in this book, "Shoeless Joe", is beautiful. And colorful. The character who is Kinsella's mother-in-law is a negative, nay-saying shrew of a woman. Kinsella says that her favorite word is "catheter". That says a lot, doesn't it. If you are a fan, you will thrill to Kinsella's ghosts coming out of the corn. I am a believer. I'm sure that I could see them. Like the main character and give credit to W.P. Kinsella here, I was born under the hit and run sign. Let me take you to another park where you can see them.

    The players materialized, one at a time, in centerfield, emerging from head-high, late-July corn that met the outfield fence. Fans new to the scene audibly gasped; spectators who had seen it before stood and applauded, but their neck hairs tingled too. It wasn't Shoeless Joe and his mates. They appear only to true believers at the Field of Dreams. These spirited players were the seniors on the Kee High baseball team being introduced out of the corn, one at a time, at their last home game, a Kee High tradition. The setting is Shooky Fink Field, Kee High's home baseball park, and for forty-five years the realm of Coach Gene Schultz, holder of the national record for wins, 1,754. A legend. It's magic and Gene Schultz is the chief magician. He retired this past season. In the course of those forty-five years, astounding things have happened. Nine men have served as President of the United States. Too many futile wars have been fought. In 1973 Coach Schultz' team was 48-0, one of his eleven State Championship teams. In 1980 he had a kid, Tom Imhoff, set a state record for hitting safely in consecutive games, forty-three. Twenty years later another of his players, Jason Crane, hit safely in forty-two straight games. I read that. I've never met Gene Schultz.

If I get to meet him, I'm going to ask how Crane's streak was stopped. Was it like the night Joe Dimaggio's fifty-six game streak ended? Ken Keltner, the Cleveland third baseman, made two difficult, back-handed stops deep at third, getting Dimaggio by a step at first both times, and on a very slow track made so by rains during the day. The closest any modern player has come to this mark is Pete Rose, who hit in forty-four straight games in 1978. Paul Molitor is seventh on the list with thirty-nine, one behind Ty Cobb's forty. Dimaggio's record will probably never be broken. First, it's an amazing feat, anytime, anywhere. But to break it, the modern player would have to succeed against how many 99mph closers out of the pen? Good as he was, Joe didn't see closers like that game after game. But how did Crane's streak stop? With a spectacular play or two? Was Schultz pulling for Crane to tie Imhoff and have it end that way? Someone knows the answers, and the mystery adds to the magic.

The baseball world of our small part of this tri-state area is incredibly inter-connected. Coach Schultz admired Max Molock, one of his coaching mentors, the same Max Molock that Mark Servais played for at

St. Mary's, and idolized. Schultz, in a newspaper article, identified Bob Welch as another mentor and influence. I played against Bob Welch when he played at Winona Cotter and at Winona State. This wonderful man died too young, perhaps of Mad Cow Disease. That would have been the ultimate bad hop, one that even Welch's soft hands couldn't handle. Baseball was just one of his athletic skills. He is in the Winona State Hall of Fame for three sports: baseball, basketball, and football. The poet A.E. Housman might have had Bob Welch in mind when he wrote:

"Smart lad to slip betimes away
From fields where glory does not stay
And early though the laurel grows
It withers quicker than the rose."

 This little literary detour reminds me that my motivation for writing this work is to memorialize, even if only a few ever read it, to name and recall and celebrate many good baseball people.
 When we talked about the cornfield in New Albin, we passed right over Harris "Shooky" Fink, the namesake of the field where Gene Schultz built his dynasty. He would say where he and Shooky and the players built the dynasty. Shooky started them young, as soon as they were strong enough to support the glove on their wrist. We have a glorious tradition here. There may be other parts of the country where baseball history is as rich or even richer, where people

have loved it more, where it also produced unique characters, their versions of Dallas Ames, Al Grob, Wimpy Miller, Boober Pariezek, and Leo Mashak. I doubt it. The inside of the cover of Leo Mashak's coffin, the one he was buried in last year, is a huge St. Louis Cardinal logo, the bat and the bird. And then there is Cootch Carroll, much mentioned to this point, a "windmill" fast-pitch pitcher in his playing days, who lubricated the arm pit of his pitching arm with Argo Corn Starch between innings, and dramatically in full view of the fans, that before he sat down to suck on a lemon.

Baseball has always had unusual characters in and around it. Maybe the game's unevenness, its separation from a clock, the intervals that lead to story-telling and bench-jockeying, the languidness of the pace, its off-centeredness, attract those of us who value those characteristics, or are burdened by them. You pick. Your answer may be determined by if you live with a true believer or not. We need to move on. But New Albin, Iowa, is a baseball shrine, a holy place.

Some of our baseball shrines were not as holy as Shooky Fink Field, nor was the air so clean and healthful. Sheldon's and the S&H (the latter not to be confused with the sporting goods part of the business) were downtown La Crosse emporiums, cigar stores they called themselves. Both establishments, one on South Fourth Street and one in the 300 block of Main Street, had huge chalk boards covering walls, and a chalk scrivener whose duty was to read and record the baseball data that clacked in on the Western Union tape, the spent tape spooling around the feet of the scrivener. Most of the major league games of the time were day games, and the scrivener would chalk in the score by innings and record the pitching changes, of which there were few compared to today, and the homeruns, on a sideboard. Milling groups of men, only men, maybe a few boys, peered at the data through the blue smoke. Fans today can follow not only the scores but even individual at-bats in any major league game, anywhere, anytime, almost in real time. The chalk boards were the best source of current information the fans had in the day. The alternative was to wait for the newspaper, which in those days was an afternoon edition with yesterday's scores. No one imagined ESPN. Enough shrines. Let's talk about a player.

We've had a number of storied baseball players in our region; any history alluded to in this work goes back to the late 40's at most. I want to give credit to a wraith, a baseball ghost, a man who may be unsung and whose exploits began at about the arbitrary time boundary I've created. Getting a handle on the athletic career of La Crosse North-Sider and Logan High School star Glen Selbo has been like going on a scavenger hunt. His high school years were in the early 40's. Say "Glen Selbo" and any local sports nut, make that old sports nut, might say "He played in the

NBA didn't he?" He did. After high school he played college basketball at Michigan for one year; he was their leading scorer that year. Then he appears at Wisconsin, becomes a Badger, and leads them to the Big 9 championship in 1947. We know that conference today as the "Big Ten". In Selbo's day it was the Big Nine, and there actually were nine teams in the conference. He was the Conference MVP. Professional basketball was in a state of flux at this time. There was a Basketball Association of America trying to get off the ground. The Toronto Huskies of that league made Glen Selbo a first round draft pick. They died a'borning. Glen then played two years with the Oshkosh All Stars of the National Basketball League, an organization that merged into the National Basketball Association, the NBA. Glen's service in the NBA amounted to 13 games with the Sheboygan Red Skins. He made his debut on November 13th, 1949. They played their home games in the 3,500 seat Sheboygan Armory. New York and Boston and the other NBA owners squeezed Sheboygan out of the NBA after their one and only year in the league. Legend has it that Red Auerbach was ejected from a game in the Armory. It was too cold to put him on the street; the dressing room was inadequate. They allowed him to stay in the stands, with a bodyguard, where he traded insults with the fans for the rest of the game. There were several franchises in the Midwest that were not good fits for the NBA. Clearly Glen Selbo was an exceptional athlete. Not many people, in any era, played professionally in two sports. Gene Conley of the Milwaukee Braves and Boston Celtics comes to mind. Glen was an exceptional basketball player. Leading scorer on one Big Nine team and key member of another school's conference championship team. Conference MVP. Drafted in the first round of one pro basketball league. Played in another, the NBA. Glen's love for basketball didn't end there. Early in his baseball career, 1951 to be exact, he played basketball with the Denver Frontier Refiners of the National Professional Basketball League. Somewhere in the background material on this man it says that he played with the Denver Nuggets. They were not in existence then, and I think a researcher confused them with the Refiners. An obituary in the Rocky Mountain News stated, sort of an oh-by-the-way, "He also played professional baseball in Texas." That's like saying Walt Disney was in the entertainment business or Jack Kennedy was a politician. Let's look at his baseball career.

Glen Selbo was a fairly big man for his time; he was listed as 6-3 and 195 pounds. Over his ten-year professional baseball career he appeared in 1,020 games and had 3,781 official at bats. His lifetime batting average was .316. He hit below .300 twice: .277 in 1948 and .292 in 1955. One source gave him credit for five years of professional baseball. It was ten years, with well over 100 games almost all of those years. He was doing double duty, baseball and basketball in the first few years of his baseball career. He hit sixteen homeruns in each of two years. For the most part, he played the outfield, but he was 19-18 lifetime as a pitcher. He started his baseball career in 1947 and finished it in 1956, ten seasons. He was 3-3 as a pitcher, appearing in 12 games, and he hit .316 as an outfielder in 121 games in 1956, his last season. He played in 133 of the 144 games his team played that year.

Glen Selbo deserves more accolades than it appears that he received. Maybe he was appropriately recognized in his day. In 1956 I was in college and playing ball in the summer leagues around here. Had Glen Selbo returned to the area and decided to play some amateur baseball at the end of his pro career, I might have had the chance to play with or against him. That would have been special. He died in Arizona in 1995 at the age of 69, just days before he was to return to his North Side roots to be inducted into the Logan High School Wall of Fame, a well-deserved if belated honor. He was a four-sport star; add tennis to football, basketball and baseball. He was an excellent student who sang in the choir and played the piano. Post-professional baseball, he served as a math teacher, a basketball coach, and an administrator in the Littleton, Colorado schools for twenty-one years.

Some evening – it won't be during a Logger game; spirits avoid crowds – but if you are in Copeland Park, and especially if there has been some rain and mist, with vapors rising off the Black River and a hint of saffron clouds presaging some clearing to the west, put yourself in an appropriate frame of mind. You may see baseball figures gliding out of the fog. You have to be a true believer. Glen Selbo should not be difficult to spot. Few of his baseball contemporaries were 6-3. Glen will be moving with the fluid grace of a basketball player. If you happen to see a short bespectacled and smiling gnome walking next to him and in animated conversation, that would be Glen Selbo's cousin, Howie Voss. The clincher would be if you had heard a voice saying "How ya doin Kid?" I believe in spirits and I think they visit sites close to their hearts. A baseball park on the North Side would be a logical place to look for him. He was one of the best we've seen here.

BASEBALL, A LOVE STORY

GLEN SELBO, center, receives the Big Ten's MVP award as Wisconsin coach Bud Foster, left, looks on in 1947.

■ Selbo

Continued from D-1

everybody knew the Selbos."

Some people still remember today.

"When I'm introduced to someone, they ask, 'Are you related to Glen Selbo?'" said Luther Selbo, the boys track coach at West Salem High School who lives in Onalaska. "He is as famous or well-known an athlete to come out of La Crosse for some time, primarily for his success at the University of Wisconsin."

Luther Selbo accepted the Wall of Fame award on behalf of his uncle. Glen Selbo was set to attend, but never made the trip to the spot of his fondest memories.

Only a few days before, Selbo died of a heart attack while backing his car out of his driveway in Sun City West, Ariz. He died May 29 at age 69.

"It was a surprise to me," said Dave Ferries, 72, a former teammate in basketball, baseball and football at Logan, who lives in La Crosse.

"It was like a shock. I read the obituary in the paper and I had to read it over a second time. I thought, 'It couldn't be Glendy.' I guess we never know. He was an awful nice fellow."

Glendon Selbo, born to Walter and Helen Selbo at 9 a.m. March 29, 1926, in La Crosse, went on to a stellar sports career at Logan, the University of Wisconsin and in professional basketball and minor-league baseball.

His biggest sports claim to fame likely was his 1947 basketball season at Wisconsin. The 6-foot-3, 195-pound senior guard was the Big Ten MVP in a season when the Badgers won the conference

The storied Glen Selbo.

Chapter 16

More Legends

There are more than a few legends in this local baseball story, and two of them have deep roots in La Crescent. George Horihan was a highly successful coach with major achievements in both the high school and American Legion programs. Out of 127 Minnesota high school coaches who have won at least 200 games, George ranks 16th with 404 wins. His teams won eleven conference titles and thirteen district or sub-section championships. He took two teams to the State Tournament, winning the consolation championship in 1999.

His American Legion teams won three State Championships, fitting for a man who served his country in the army for six years. In 2001 he was named the Minnesota American Legion Coach of the

Year, not an insignificant award in that Minnesota has the second-most Legion teams of all the fifty states. In addition to developing players and winning games, George probably put an equal amount of time into raising funds and building and maintaining a jewel of a playing field, now named George Horihan Field. It is a rare high school baseball coach that doesn't also serve as a groundskeeper, and George was the best. Earl Seaton Football Stadium is adjacent to the baseball complex. Although Earl was a fine baseball player, he made his mark in La Crescent as a football coach, athletic director, and philosopher. Steve Mau, a former La Crescent football coach, testified that he once went to his boss, Earl the Athletic Director, and confessed that he was depressed over being 0-5 at that point of the season. Earl, a navy combat veteran, told him that when your ship is shot full of holes, as Earl's once was, and sinking, that's the time to be depressed. Go back to work.

One of the kindest and most thoughtful men I've ever known, Earl Seaton died recently. When the end was near, he had to be taken from his home by ambulance. He asked the driver to go by the stadium so he could see his name on the press box one last time. I hope that George Horihan goes by the baseball field often and for many years, and that each time he takes satisfaction in seeing his name emblazoned on the baseball scoreboard. There are hundreds of former players of his who won't need the score board to remember him. If you are new to the area, or if you only knew him from a distance, this man was a major contributor to the La Crescent baseball scene. Acknowledge him if you see him.

Rick Boyer's story could be a chapter in Ripley's Believe it or Not. He is beginning his fourteenth year as the La Crescent High School head baseball coach, having taken over when George Horihan retired. He has won 244 games and lost 103. He guided the Lancers to the State Championship over Fergus Falls in 2009, that tournament contested at Dick Putz Field in St. Cloud. He brought the Lancers right back to the 2010 championship game at Target Field, home of the Minnesota Twins, where they lost to St. Cloud Cathedral in the championship game. In total there were five trips to the State Tournament. Rick would be the first to tell you that a lot of credit goes to the program that George Horihan built, brick by brick and roll of sod by roll of sod, and to the school and community assistant coaches and supporters. For a long time, Rick was one of those helpers. He started coaching baseball in the Middle School in 1976, thirty-nine years ago.

His name and even his face might be familiar to you. He has looked down at us from billboards throughout the region, touting the surgical excellence that repaired his shoulder, damaged by injury and worn by throwing what might have been one million batting practice pitches, had anyone been counting, when machines weren't in use for that purpose. This man at 62 is still playing amateur baseball with the young folks, and at a high level. He played baseball for Coach Rollie Johnson at La Crescent High School, class of 1970, and for Coach Bill Terry at UWL, where teammates included Ed Servais, Mike Dee, Andy Christensen, Rich Kaiser, and Jerry Augustine.

Boyer's resume includes having played for Dakota, La Crescent, Stoddard, the La Crosse 35er's, and Rollie Christensens' Old Style Lagers. Over the years he has loaned himself out for tournament games for Eau Claire teams, New Albin, and to a 45 and older team in the Quad Cities. He was an elder statesman there. Several of those "and older" teams picked him up to play in fall national tournaments in Arizona and Florida, at the individual player's own expense. He got hits off both Mike Caldwell and Bill "Spaceman" Lee in one of those geriatric tournaments. He served two years as the manager of the La Crosse Loggers where future major leaguers Vic Black, Eric Thames, and Brett Jackson played for him. In my conversation with him, I couldn't name a single local baseball personage that he hadn't played with or against, coached, or saw play. (He got quick-pitched by Kozidowski too. I'm mad all over.) Legend is not too strong a term.

There is a character in La Crosse who has had a large impact on the local baseball scene, and he is neither player nor manager. This story began about twenty years ago when Jim Geissner, Director of Human Resources for the City of La Crosse and a big baseball fan, was pained by the political scene he saw every day. Jim saw a region, an interdependent mix of political subdivisions that needed each other, often taking their bats and balls and going home rather than playing nicely together. What would happen if they all went to a ball game together?

In just a few years Geissner's idea turned into the largest community day that the Milwaukee Brewers enjoy. It's a spine-tingler to see more than thirty large motor coaches carrying 1,500 area fans to Miller Park. There is a huge area set up for a picnic; traditionally the Moose Club sets up the evening before and serves the meal. I don't know that anyone calls it "homecoming", but it serves that purpose. It's also made Jim Geissner a popular person with the Brewer event staff. Not too many people buy 1,500 seats for a game.

What kind of good karma was it in 2007 when the area's own Damian Miller hit a three-run, walk-off home run in the bottom of the eleventh inning to beat Cincinnati on La Crosse Day? In his very next game he hit two home runs, one a grand slam, and had a record-sharing seven RBI's. It would be good if we could say that partly as a result of La Crosse Days, when local constituencies take turns singing the anthem and throwing out first pitches and sharing the love, we now have regional police and fire departments, French Island is at peace, and no one wants a toll bridge over the river. We haven't come that far. Yet.

BASEBALL, A LOVE STORY

We have come a long way with American Legion baseball here in La Crosse. Legion baseball was born in South Dakota in 1925. The Roy L. Vingers Post 52, La Crosse, started their program in 1933 and it has been running strong for eighty-one years. La Crosse has been the state champion ten times, more than any other post. Add to that nine runner-up finishes. Appleton's record is next best, but locals like to say that is because their long-time coach, Don Hawkins, is a La Crosse native who played for Post 52 in the 1950 and 1951 seasons.

Over the years there have been twenty-three coaches, six of whom came through the ranks as players for the local team: Bill Meyer, Boober Parizek, Ken Barrett, Jim Mason, Dave Bruha, and Andy Christensen. There have been thirty-eight father-son combinations who have worn the local Legion uniform. Actually, there were more combinations than that because there have been thirty-eight fathers, and fifty sons. Jim Squier had four sons play and Dick Ghelfi three.

La Crosse was the state champion three consecutive years, 1980 to 1982. That was matched only by Janesville, 1974- 1976, and Oshkosh, 1953-1955. The 1942 Post 52 team, state champions, advanced to the national regional finals in Russell, Kansas, where they were eventually beaten by the St. Louis team, whose catcher was one Yogi Berra. Babe Rieber pitched for that La Crosse team. Two years later he was in the 87th Infantry Division under

General George Patton. The stakes were considerably higher in Europe. Babe's sons Ron and Gordie played Legion baseball here, as did Gordie's son, Ryan. The baseball community in La Crosse is wonderfully intertwined. Babe Rieber's daughter Teri is married to Tom Juan, a Central High and Post 52 star, and their son Bobby's pedigree includes the Loggers and the University of Minnesota.

Legion baseball has expanded over the years, adding classifications and levels, allowing more communities and more athletes to enjoy the great game of baseball. I hope many of them were as thrilled as I was to get their Legion uniform. Rod Martin handed me my first one, scratchy wool with the Legion emblem on the chest. I think I slept in it the day I got it.

Powerhouse baseball programs, and Post 52 is one, almost always have a Promethian figure, someone who knows the game well, can teach it, and is willing to sacrifice time and even personal treasure to build a tradition. Jim Coonan is that man for Post 52. He served as the coach for nineteen consecutive years, 1976 through 1994, winning five state championships in that period. Andy Christensen, a legend in the making, kept the fire burning. Prometheus, by the way, was the mythological being who brought fire from Heaven as a gift for man. Cooney and Christensen brought a fire for baseball. Andy coached the 1995 and 1996 teams and then hooked up with Coonie as co-coach in 1997. They have been at it ever since, bringing Jim Coonan's years of service to thirty-seven.

I stopped at the Legion clubrooms one Friday afternoon to check some facts. I knew Coonie would be there prepping for the regular Friday fund-raising fish fries. He was. So was Andy Christensen. And Tom Juan. And Bobby Juan. And others. The research lost its focus and spiraled into baseball stories, a risk one takes in talking to Coonie. Max Molock's name came up again. Remember, Mark Servais played for him and idolized him. He was a mentor for Gene Schultz. Coonie had been one of Max Molock's assistants at one time. Jim Coonan's fingerprints seem to be on a lot of baseball programs in the area. Suddenly I was hearing about a St. Mary's baseball trip that included a game against Vanderbilt in Nashville, Tennessee. I didn't hear about the game. I heard about Max knocking on Coonie's motel room door at 11 o'clock at night recruiting him for a search for chili dogs. "Irene doesn't let me eat them at home."

Irene was a true partner to Max by the way. They danced the polka every Friday night in the off-season. She threw out the first pitch of the first game every season. Max finished coaching in 1983. Irene died. Then Max died in 1984, of the proverbial broken heart. There is an old baseball story that I know you have heard, but I need to tell it here to set up the finish.

A spirit of a deceased baseball man appears to

one of his former teammates. Let's call the receiver of this visit Bill. The shock passes and the visit begins. Finally Bill, curious about eternity, asks the question: "Is there baseball in Heaven?"

"Oh, yes, and it is great. The infields are pool-table smooth. There are no bad hops. There is no wind and no bad sun-fields and no rain delays. There are enough clouds to give perspective on fly balls. The temperature is always perfect. If you hit one on the handle, there are no bees in the bat. The umpires never make a bad call. Since this is Heaven, no one quick pitches either, I will add."

"That's great."

"Well, there is one problem here."

"And that is?"

"Bill, You are catching Saturday, and batting third."

I am trying to imagine what it would be like, many years from now, to be able to sit in with Dallas Ames, Wimpy Miller, Max Molock, and Jim Coonan, just to listen to their baseball stories. Heaven. And all the chili dogs you want.

Back row: Coach Jim Coonan, Joe Fischer, Doug Wright, Brandt Freitag, Jim Gilbert, Scott Bakkum, Eric Brieske, David Buckley, Mike Murak, Coach Jay Adams.
Front row: Jason Bahr, Monte Nunemacher, George Williams, Tim Quilling, Todd Delaney, Scott Bagniefski, Mike Butler.

One of Jim Coonan's State Championship Teams. Third from left front row is George Williams, major league catcher.

Chapter 17

Roll Call

When I told my wife about my plans for Chapter 17, she gave me her advice. "Don't". Over the years I have learned that I disregard her counsel at some peril. There was the unfortunate incident on the Don Ho Freeway in Bangkok involving a rogue taxi driver, two rogue taxi drivers, actually, one of whom had run out of gas, and the rope connecting them. At 2:00 am in the morning. Then there was the tout who lied about an attraction being closed, and who offered to guide us elsewhere. Yes, and the pickpocket attempt in Amsterdam. Or was it Copenhagen? I suppose she would insist that I mention the contretemps the day that Leonid Brezhnev and our very young family visited Washington D.C. on the very same day. Could have been an international incident. So I struggled with her advice about Chapter 17. She held her position. "Don't do it".

But I am going to do it. My plan is to list alphabetically in an appendix nearly 500 people meaningful to me in a baseball or fast pitch context. It is not an index because not all of them appear in the book. I just don't want to forget them. It brings me pleasure and good memories to list them. I understand my wife's rationale. Surely I am going to overlook someone, someone who means more to me than most people on the list perhaps. That will be hurtful and embarrassing.

My defense is this. I am pegging the over-under on the number of people who will read this book at fifty. I am betting under. Those forty-five or so who do read the book will fall into two distinct groups: those whose names are in the appendix and those whose names are not, the latter group having no expectation of being there. No harm no foul. I will put my contact information at the end of the list, and if someone feels slighted he (or she) could contact me and I would abjectly and sincerely apologize. It's possible that I would have to end up saying, as I did with those other events, "It seemed like a good idea at the time."

It will be good, though, to get a decent night's sleep again. For months now I have come awake in the middle of the night because a name swam up from my subconscious, a name that should be included in the appendix. I'd fumble in the dark for something to write with and on and blindly record the name. In the morning whatever I had written was illegible. It looked like a prescription. It was as though I had written in tongues. I couldn't detect a vowel, which might have given me a contextual clue. It might as well have been the name on the back of a jersey on a Russian hockey player.

It reminded me of the Woody Allen bit when he went into the bank and handed the teller a holdup note. I need to pause and digress here in case any of the forty-five readers happen to be young. A teller was a person who worked behind a counter in a bank, often a cage-like station, where customers could slide cash and checks back and forth in banking transactions. The teller might take your cash and passbook, deposit the money, and hand back your up-to-date savings book. Tellers have become nearly extinct. Today you could pull the pin and roll a hand grenade across the lobby floor and there would be few or no casualties. Not so in the day. The tellers were wall to wall.

But back to Woody and the teller. She looks at the note, at him, and asks "What does this say?" Mr. Allen looks nervously over both shoulders, one at a time, and tells her " It says put the money in the bag and don't sound the alarm."

She can't read the note any better than I can read the ghost name written in the dark. "That's not a 'p' " she says. Turning to the teller next to her, she says "Ethel, does that look like a 'p' to you?". Meanwhile, Woody Allen looks very nervous.

BASEBALL, A LOVE STORY

Some of my middle-of-the night insights did result in names. Kaydon Rudie was one. I'm not sure how he spelled his first name, but I have the sound right. We were probably about eleven years old. I would ride my bike across Lang Drive or the Causeway to play Recreation Department baseball at Copeland. Kaydon was a player there too and he invited me to his birthday lunch. It was just he and I and his mother in a neat and clean apartment over the Sweet Shop on Caledonia Street. Did he invite me the same day we had lunch? I don't remember bringing a present. That was about the essence of our interaction, but I don't want to forget Kaydon, or anyone else. Forgive me if I have.

Appendix

A is for Aaron. He did it without steroids.

Abbegglen, Jim
Abraham, Bill
Ahern, Dan
Alberts, Frank
Ames, Dallas *(Amo)*
Ammerman, Gar
Ankney, John
Augustine, Jerry
Azzinaro, Sam

B is for Banks. Let's play two.

Badzinski, Joel
Banasik, Steve
Barnes, Carl
Barnes, Ron
Bartel, Joe
Bateman, Bob
Bauer, Gordy
Beck, Ken
Beck, Roger
Beckley, Dan
Bendel, Bob
Bendel, Jerry
Benedict, Dave
Benedict, Dean
Benson, Roger
Beranek, Bill
Beranek, Clarence *(Swish)*

Besl, Jim
Besl, Tom
Blaken, Tom
Blank, Hugh
Blank, Steve *(Harv)*
Blanchard, Ken
Boardman, Dennis
Boma, Charlie
Bott, Jim
Boyer, Rick
Bradburn, Dick
Brandt, Bill
Brault, Orv
Brietbach, Dick
Brose, Brian
Brose, Frank *(Bubs)*
Brose, John
Bruha, Dave
Bruha, Paul
Burt, Terry

**C is for Clemente.
He died helping others.**

Callaway, Larry
Callum, Rich
Campbell, Lloyd
Carroll, Robert *(Cootch)*
Chapiewski, Wilfred
Chapman, Steve
Christensen, Andy
Christensen, Rollo
Christensen, Steve
Cleary, Ken *(Dad)*
Clements, Dave *(Squeek)*
Coady, Mike
Collins, Dave
Collins, Terry
Colburn, Dave *(Whitey)*
Conyers, Doug

Goodell, Chris
Gooderum, Ruben
Gordineer, Pete
Grabhorn, Cary
Grams, Herb
Grinke, Allan
Grob, Al
Grob, Gary
Groggins, Dynamite
Gruntzel, Ron
Groth, Don
Groth, Ron
Groves, L. Peter
Guentz, Jerry

H is for Hardy, J.J., always underrated.

Hackett, Dick
Haddad, Norm
Halaska, Bob
Hallingstad, Wayne

Halverson, Chut
Halverson, Jim
Halverson, Mike
Hammes, Dave
Hanifl, Jerry
Happel, Ken
Harebo, Elwood
Harnisch, Babe
Harnisch, Tom
Haupert, Michael
Hawkins, Don
Heiderscheidt, Pat
Henley, Jim
Herrman, Stan
Hertzfeldt, Don
Hilbo, Jim
Hoadley, Clete
Hockenberry, Chuck
Hoffland, Bill
Hogden, Larry
Hogden, Vince (2)

Hole, Dan
Horihan, George
Huebner, Walt
Huinker, Art
Hundt, Bob
Hyland, Bill

I is for Ichiro, a gift from Japan.

Imhoff, Tom
Iverson, Dave
Iverson, Roger

J is for Jackson, Mr. October.

Jacobson, Don *(Red)*
Jacobus, Blair
Jacobus, Ron
Jacques, Leon
Jenkins, Darrell

Jennings, Don *(Red)*
Jensen, Dale
Jirsa, Gene
Jirsa, Jim
Johnson, Earl
Johnson, Ed
Johnson, Everett
Johnson, Rollie
Juan, Bobby
Juan, Tom

K is for Kaline, Albert William, Mr. Tiger.

Kaiser, Bob
Kaiser, Carrol
Kaiser, Rich (2)
Kaliban, Bob *(Mr. Tidy Bowl)*
Kapanke, Ben
Kapanke, Dan
Kapanke, Elizabeth

Kapanke, Ruth
Kapellas, Tom
Kapsch, Pat
Keenan, Dick
Kezman, Bill
Kime, Bob
(the Professor)
Kipper, Thornton
Klawitter, Tom
Knutson, Jim
Koebel, Jim
Koeller, Jeff *(Effie)*
Kohlwey, Bruce
Kohnert, Pete
Konrath, Dave
Korn, Joe,
Kowalkowski, Bruno
Kowitz, Norm
Kressin, Dick
Kroll, Derrick
Kroner, Ray
Kroner, Russ

Krull, Jack
Kusick, Craig

L is for Larkin.
Shortstop.

Larkin, Ed
Larkin, Gary
Larkin, Tom (2)
Larkin, Willie
Larson, Jim
Larson, Tom
Lathrop, Bill
Lathrop, Ned
Lawrynk, Larry
Lawrynk, Rock
Lee, Phil
Lepsch, Ron
Lindvig, Harlan
Loomis, Bud
Loomis, Dick
Loomis, Dave

Lottes, Wayne
Lukas, Jeff
Lund, Russ *(Pug)*
Lusk, Dave *(Bear)*
Lyons, Art
Lyons, Steve

M is for Musial, Stan the Man.

Mahlum, Bud
Marson, Jeff
Martin, Doug
Martin, Rod
Maringer, Bob
Mashak, Leo
Mason, Jim *(Banana)*
Mattes, Jarvis
McConaghy, Steve
McCurdy, Stan
McEldowney, Todd
McIntyre, Jim

McPeak, Dave
McQuillan, Paul
Mears, Wally
Mehren, Bob
Meinking, Harry
Mickelson, Dick
Mickelson, Steve
Miller, Alvin *(Wimpy)*
Miller, Damian
Miller, Tom
Mischkl, Willie
Molock, Max
Moran, Horace

N is for the Neikro boys, Joe and Phil.

Nate, Bucko
Nehring, Merlin *(Hambone)*
Nelson, Dave

Nelson, Earl
Nelson, Ken
New, Jack
Nockles, Jack
Noelke, Mike
Noelke, Tom
Noonan, Frank
Neumeister, Jim
Nustad, Pete

O is for Oliva, Tony, if only his knees had been good.

Oelke, Loren
Oleson, Vern
Olson, Shorty
Olson, Vern
Ondell, Jess
Opsadl, Dick
Osgood, Gene
Ottavi, Joe

Ott, Dick
Otto, Jack

P is for Paige, what might have been...

Pamperin, John
Papenfuss, Dick
Papenfuss, Lyle (Slats)
Paul, John +
Paul, Lee
Pavela, John
Pavela, Steve
Peregrine, Dick
Peterson, John
Peth, Dick
Peth, Don
Pfenning, Ray
Pfenning, Mike
Pickett, Jim (2)
Pongratz, Fred

(Fritz)
Potts, Cy
Potts, Gene *(Tiny)*
Powell, Keith
Powers, Perry
Preeshl, Jim
Preidel, Gene
Preidel, Jim
Pulver, Ben

Q is for Quisenberry, out of the pen.

Quinn, Jim
Quinn, Jimmy
Quinn, Romey

R is for Ripken, who else?

Radatz, Dick Jr
Radde, Bruce

Rego, Mike
Reiman, Tony
Reindl, Tom
Renslo, Tom
Ressler, Wayne
Richards, Billy
Richardson, Joe
Rieber, Roland *(Babe)*
Rieber, Gordie
Rieber, Ron
Rieber, Ryan
Rieder, Winston *(Windy)*
Riegard, Tom
Rudie, Kaydon

S is for Scherzer, Max, Cy Young winner who played for the Loggers.

Sandmire, Roger

Schaefer, Ed
Schelbe, Bill
Schiffer, Frank
Schilling, Alger *(Corky)*
Schmidt, Tom
Schmitz, Duane
Schmitz, Virgil
Schneyer, Bob *(Red)*
Schreiber, Billy
Schreiber, Bobby
Schroeder, Bob
Schroeder, Clumsy
Schubert, Jerry
Schultz, Gene
Schultz, Rocky
Schuman, John
Schwertferger, Robert
Sciborski, Bob
Seaton, Earl
Seidel, Dick

Seidel, R J
Selbo, Glen
Servais, Ed
Servais, Eric
Servais, Mark
Servais, Scott
Severson, Butch
Shea, Arnie
Shea, Sam
Shelton, John *(Rooster)*
Shepardson, Ron *(Shep)*
Shrake, Joe
Skemp, Bill
Skogen, Barb
Skogen, Dave
Skogen, Mark
Sladky, George
Smith, Bud
Smith, Danny
Smith, Dick
Smith, Don

Solie, Arlen
Soller, Mike
Spink, Bob
Spink, Dick
Squire, Chalky
Stafford, John
Steenerson, Bill
Steffes, Cal
Steffes, Jon
Steigerwald, Bob
Steigerwald, Joe
Stellick, Jack
Stendahl, Dewey
Stone, Ron
Strittmater, Dave
Stuhr, Jeff
Stuhr, Jerry
Stuhr, Paul
Sullivan, Tom
Sutton, Mark
Swan, James
Synoground, Rolf

T is for Tulowitzki, the rock of the Rockies.

Tanke, Buck
Temp, Jim *(Dumbo)*
Terry, Bill
Thomas, Steve
Thompson, Greg *(Rocky)*
Thompson, Orrie
Tischer, Bud
Tischer, Tom
Toepel, Al
Tooke, Bob
Tooke, Pat
Thornton, Frank
Thornton, Matt
Timmons, George
Tremain, Ron
Trott, Ken

Twite, Bruce (Guffy)

Twite, Ralph

Twite, Richard

Twite, Ron

Tylka, Dale

V is for Viola, Frank (Sweet Music).

Valley, Roger

Van Ert, Wayne

Veghlan, Arnie (Judge)

Vickroy, Bill

Vinger, Don

Vingers, Len

Voboril, Bill

Vollmer, John

Von Voorhis, George

Voss and Clark (Mohawk middle infielders)

Voss, Howie

Voss, Mike

Voss, Petesy

W is for Williams, Ted, the greatest hitter of all.

Wais, Bob

Walsh, Pat (Flip)

Wanner, Jim

Washburn, Jarrod

Weber, Jack

Weber, Pete

Weibel, Larry

Weigent, Charlie

Weiland, Dick (Rugged)

Welch, Bob

Weldy, Dave

Werth, Jim

Wetzel, Orv

Whipple, Art
Whiting John
Wilhelm, Ron
Wilkins, Sonny
Willhite, Bob *(Scooter)*
Williams, George
Winter, Dick
Wittmerhaus, Art
Witzke, Terry
Woelhoefer, Huzzy
Wohlert, Darrell
Wolf, Don
Wolfe, Bob

Woodworth, Dick
Wright, Dick *(Garney)*
Wuensch, Lloyd *(Red)*
Wuest, Paul *(Pip)*
Wuest, Tom

Z is for Zarilla, Al, of the Red Sox and others.

Zahn, Acky
Zielke, Corrine
Zielke, Pat

BILL LEONARD

ABOUT THE AUTHOR

Bill Leonard was born under the hit and run sign, a zodiac marker first identified by W.P. Kinsella, author of "Shoeless Joe". He played sandlot, recreation department, high school, American Legion, college, and town team baseball. He coached the game and he umpired.

His dad was a wonderful father, but they never played catch and he knows of only a single relative, Uncle Wayne, who ever played baseball, and that was before his time. Nonetheless, baseball is in the makeup of his genes. No one had to introduce him to the game or encourage him to play. It was as predetermined as the salmon swimming from the ocean up the smallest stream.

He knew instinctively the feel of the game: the solid, hollow-sounding explosion of the barrel of the bat on the baseball, the thwack of the short hop into the glove; the sounds of the game: the chatter of the sandlot players, the pop of the catcher's mitt enveloping a fast ball, the strike call of the umpire; the smells of the game: the lanolin rubbed into the pocket of the glove and the red-hot on the arm, the cloud arising from the rosin bag, the damp sweat in the leather margin of the mask; the sights of the game: the white ball landing on the green grass between two outfielders, the ballet around second base on the double play, the third base coach going through a set of signs.

He played rounders and stickball and he threw a hard rubber ball against the wall of Fredrickson's Food Store until it hurt to lift his arm. He chose to catch because of some latent strain of masochism. "Love Story" is an attempt to record those sensations before they are gone.

BASEBALL, A LOVE STORY

Made in the USA
San Bernardino, CA
22 March 2015